GIVE & GET EMPLOYER BRANDING

GIVE

&

GET

EMPLOYER BRANDING

Repel the Many and Compel the Few
with Impact, Purpose and Belonging

BRYAN ADAMS & **CHARLOTTE MARSHALL**

HOUNDSTOOTH
PRESS

GIVE & GET EMPLOYER BRANDING

Repel the Many and Compel the Few with Impact, Purpose and Belonging

ISBN 978-1-5445-0708-8 *Hardcover*

    978-1-5445-0706-4 *Paperback*

    978-1-5445-0707-1 *Ebook*

To Harrison, Sydney, and Cameron.

You give us so much joy (most of the time) and make all of life's trials and tribulations more than worthwhile. It's all for you guys. We love you.

CONTENTS

———

FOREWORD

BY GERRY CRISPIN[1]

"The most important kind of freedom is to be what you really are.

You trade in your reality for a role.

You trade in your sense for an act.

You give up your ability to feel, and in exchange, put on a mask.

There can't be any large-scale revolution until there's a personal revolution, on an individual level.

It's got to happen inside first."

—JIM MORRISON

---

1   Gerry Crispin stays grounded by engaging a community of friends and colleagues every day—actively promoting the notion that talent acquisition is the "point of the spear" of HR. Every stakeholder in the hiring process, especially candidates, must have their basic needs addressed. Gerry founded CareerXroads in 1996 to encourage the transformation of hiring into the twenty-first century. Today, with his business partner, Chris Hoyt, CareerXroads is a premier member-driven community of Talent leadership teams from a hundred-plus major firms who are devoted to learning from and helping one another improve.

As a card-carrying radical student of the recruiting land-scape for more than fifty years, I could simply write a few sentences, implore you to read *Give and Get*, and move on.

After reading Bryan and Charlotte's draft, I'm compelled to explain why it is important for each of us to do much more than that.

More than the enjoyable intellectual components of the *Give and Get* model, there are truly revolutionary possibilities afoot here. Not new in the "Aha!" sense, but in the way these two authors present their ideas—systematically, discussed case by case, and always, always doable, so we know that we, too, can execute them successfully.

Give and Get offers us the means to change our piece of the landscape going forward, not just in degree but also in kind. What we must bring to this party is the choice to step up to the promise you find here.

Let me digress for a moment with a personal story and a few notions about my interpretation of revolutionary in the context of recruiting.

Early in my adult life, while in grad school, I was fortu-nate to have an epiphany about the choices I would make for the rest of my life. Needing money to support myself (backbreaking loans were not available then), I scored a job at my alma mater, Stevens Institute of Technology, as an assistant career services professional.

With my freshly minted engineering degree and a couple of psych courses under my belt, I thought this gig was going to be a piece of cake. I interviewed each graduating student, engineers and scientists all, advising on the basics of comportment, résumé writing, the top ten dumb questions every recruiter asks, and then sent them off to interview. The average student had five to ten offers, and no one left without a job. Piece of cake. Did I also mention that at the time, the Vietnam War was raging and engineers as well as graduate students had deferments? (Until they didn't, but then I also scored a 285 in the lottery.) In hindsight, I lived a pretty privileged life, albeit one that was also quite naive.

One day while peering out my office window (we were in Hoboken on the Hudson River with a magnificent view of Manhattan), an alumnus, approximately forty years old, came into my office seeking help to find a job. He was a mess, depressed to the point that I feared he would do something rash. Long story short, he had worked for a major defense contractor for the nineteen years since he had graduated from Stevens and had just been laid off. His pension would have vested in six months! No pension. Nada. He was given two weeks' severance. He had no nest egg. He stood to lose everything. (You read that right.

Laws have changed, but this was a more common practice in the predigital universe.) There is a shock that comes to all of us when you suddenly realize that the world isn't fair. If you don't own your career, your employer is unlikely to be as loyal as they expect you to be. You get the picture. My bubble burst.

And needless to say, my inadequacy in supplying professional support intellectually and emotionally to that alumnus was evident to me such that I can still dredge up the pain on a moment's notice, but that isn't the end of my story.

I went to my boss and pleaded for the training to learn how to help others. But really, it was more for myself. The realization, perhaps for the first time, of how few business decisions would be made that considered *my* career and *my* life's investments individually over, say, those of the stockholders, was unsettling. I needed a new mental model for imagining the possibilities I should be aware of for jobs, careers, and life. The truth is that most people, out of ignorance or fear, still fail to ask themselves the questions that define them until they are halfway through their lives. Employers almost never serve up what isn't asked. Why risk it?

At the time, the bookstore shelves were not packed with great career-related books. *What Color Is Your Parachute?*

by Richard Bolles was the best of the lot in those days and was barely in its third edition (yes, he was once considered "radical"). Luckily, he was offering a weeklong experience for career service professionals nearby.

It was on the second day of his training course that Richard asked each of us to write our obituary. We had fifteen minutes. It took me five. I read it over and thought, "What an asshole this person was." I wrote another. And another. And another. Same result. Two weeks after the training, I finally wrote the paragraphs that satisfied me. I folded it up and put it in my wallet. For the next thirty years, I pulled it out every time I had a life, career, or job challenge. When I was fifty-two, I brought it out for the last time and realized...I was that person.

If you are thinking the point of the story is about what I wrote, you've missed what would constitute a revolution in recruiting.

Revolution is a misused term. Arguably, it is the most common metaphor for how we translate the confusion of change around us. Over the years, it has become so ubiquitous that it is applied to any change—nearly forty thousand book titles on Amazon use that word in their title.

It's time we get back to the basic *Webster Dictionary* definition of revolution: "The forcible overthrow of a...social order, in favor of a new system."

Implicit in this definition and especially in the context of recruiting, it is not just about making tools, concepts, and models like those available in *Give and Get*. It is combining them with candidates and recruiting leaders who step up to shift the focus away from doing more of the same thing to something completely different. From sales to informed choice. From screening candidates to candidates screening us.

When *Give and Get* advances the notion that we need to "repel the many and compel the few" around meaningful issues such as aligning to a candidates' purpose, their impact, and sense of belonging with full transparency, they are fomenting real change ("in kind," not degree), about how we attract, engage, screen, and select the pool of prospects. The center of gravity of the hiring decision shifts dramatically.

Thomas Kuhn explains in his book *The Structure of Scientific Revolutions* that a true revolution shifts from the existing problems available for scrutiny to challenge the basic notion of what is a problem. These changes foster controversies that become defining characteristics of a new order.

When *Give and Get* focuses on telling the truth to ensure candidates can make informed decisions, traditional notions of who oversees selection decisions and the order in which those decisions can be made are turned upside down. This is frightening to traditional models.

If you bow to an employer's traditional notions of reducing risk, putting the best spin on the work, and manufacturing "engaging" content at the cost of a deeper understanding and support of how good choices are made, you will read *Give and Get*, and perhaps nod agreement with little to no incentive to apply what you might learn—save whining about why "they" aren't letting you accomplish what's possible. Save your money.

If instead you apply first what you learn to your own purpose, your desire for impact, and sense of belonging and examine what you are willing to risk in that light, you might then imagine the possibilities and choose to influence "them."

Israeli professors Noam Tirosh and Amit Schejter said it best in their 2017 digital blog, *Who Benefits from the So-Called New Media Revolution*:

> "Revolutions are not mere changes in a perceived reality; instead, they are an inherent alteration of the foundation of reality."

PREFACE

———

The struggle in life is what some people fear the most. In others, it's what brings them alive and drives them forward. Either way, *adversity* is the most tangible link between who we are and explaining why anything has meaning to us.

Nothing in life that is worthwhile is easy. Right?

When we evaluate the value of something, we need to know how hard it will be to achieve it, or it's virtually impossible to know whether we want to pursue it. Will the juice be worth the squeeze?

This is as true for deciding whether to buy a new car as it is for deciding on your next career move. It's true for staying in a relationship, or learning a new skill, language, or sport.

How hard will it be to achieve it?

How badly do I want or need it?

When something is easy to obtain, we lower the value

attached to it. Think back to when you turned sixteen. Did your parents hand you the keys to a shiny new car, or did they make you save up and use your own hard-earned money to achieve car ownership? Chances are, if you worked for months and months to save up, you appreciated that car a lot more than if it were simply given to you.

It's no different when it comes to our careers. Specifically, when we're deciding whether to stay or join an organization, there are three main buckets of adversity we're looking to satisfy: purpose, impact, and belonging.

1. How will I be able to fulfill my personal purpose at this organization?
2. How will I be able to create impact at this organization?
3. How will I be able to feel like I belong at this organization?

To assess and evaluate the answers to each of these closely clustered questions, we first must gauge how *hard* it will be to achieve each one.

Sometimes we're assessing, "Is the wall too high to scale?" Other times we're assessing, "Is the wall sufficiently high to bring meaning and value to my climb?" In both cases, we need to understand the size of the struggle.

The beauty of employer brand is that everyone is different. Our tolerance, threshold, and endurance for situations, demands, and expectations of a company vary. That's why you can use your employer brand as a smart filter to compel people who are well suited to your organization to apply, and at the same time encourage people unsuited to your culture to stay away.

Some people will be challenged and engaged by the adversity within your organization. They will find your expectations and demands to be fair and possibly even revel in the idea that they can cope where others could not.

Other candidates, however, will be turned off, dissuaded and completely deterred from applying for any roles you may have.

This is how you "repel the many and compel the few" with the same message.

We've written this book to help you discover your unique brand of adversity and to show you how the struggles within your organization hold the power to elevate the value of the upside of joining and staying with your organization.

Together, we will explore and discover the intrinsic link between the effort, commitment, and sacrifice required to feel the impact, purpose, and belonging you can find within.

What's more, we will follow a simple approach to using these insights to craft a meaningful employee value proposition (EVP) based on a mutual value exchange that we call the *Give and Get*.

This approach is different to the conventional employer branding methodology that focuses solely on the opportunities, benefits, and strengths of joining your organization. We believe your employer brand and EVP become much more effective when you couple the strengths, benefits, and opportunities with the adversity people must embrace to thrive within your organization.

After all, it's your specific brand of difficult that makes you different.

Owning it could be the very thing that helps you attract (and keep) more than your fair share of top talent, while dissuading the rest from overwhelming your talent funnel with unqualified applications.

INTRODUCTION

———

"Your future hasn't been written yet. No one's has. Your future is whatever you make it. So, make it a good one."

—DOC EMMETT BROWN

In 1942, World War II hung in the balance.

A small fleet of bombers, flying over German occupied territory, were getting shot down on multiple bombing runs. More needed to be done to protect and reinforce the planes to increase the survival rate, or else the fleet would soon deplete to nothing.

But there was a problem. They couldn't afford to reinforce the entire plane. It would take too long, cost too much, and armor would add far too much additional weight to the plane.

The challenge became where to add a small amount of strategically placed armor without weighing it down.

An army of the world's best engineers, researchers, and analysts set to work.

Every plane in the fleet was forensically analyzed, every bullet hole was cataloged and mapped to a big data representation of where the planes were being hit the most on their bombing runs. As you can see, most of the damage was in the fuselage and the wings.

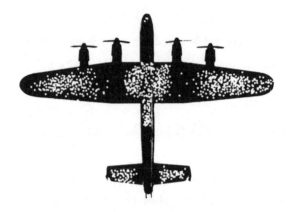

In the eleventh hour of the project, just as the order was being created to reinforce the planes in these places, a scientist named Abraham Wald joined the project team.

He declared, "Gentlemen, you have all researched and mapped the wrong data." These are planes that survived, he explained. These bullet holes provide us with precisely where the planes are capable of being shot multiple times and still make it back successfully.

They needed to analyze the planes that did not make it back.

By reversing the data, looking at the gaps and where data has not yet been gathered, they discovered the cockpit and engines needed reinforcement, not the wings or the fuselage.

Many say Abraham Wald and his counterintuitive thinking is what delivered victory in World War II.

EMPLOYER BRAND INDUSTRY

The employer brand industry is looking in the wrong place. Traditionally, we have been analyzing the wrong "bullet holes" in our search to find what makes us unique and compelling.

If you want to attract, engage, and retain top talent and deliver a victorious outcome for your organization, it's time to look elsewhere.

As an industry, we're obsessed with finding the "authentic" strengths, benefits, and opportunities within our organizations.

But if we want to truly define a fully authentic employee experience, we need to seek out the adversity within our organization and craft a balance value exchange rather than a one-way broadcast of our strengths.

We would like to bring the days of merely bragging the

truth about how great we are to a close. Even if it's true, your strengths, benefits, and opportunities aren't enough on their own to constitute an effective employer brand and employee value proposition (EVP).

After thirty combined years of developing, launching, and driving employer brand and EVPs around the world, we are sharing our experience to help you build and deploy your next employer brand in a simple, yet powerful, way. As a result, it is our hope that you take what you learn from this book and apply it to define the employee experience of your organization in a way that inspires, moves, and resonates with your audience. Most of all, we hope it educates them and allows them to make a balanced, informed personal life decision that works out well for them and well for you, too.

When you're done, we want you to feel confident that you have bottled the magic of your organization, that you have found what makes you different, and that you have defined what makes you special. We want you to craft and share stories that create an emotional connection between your company, its people, and its candidates. And we want you to turn your entire workforce into a team of ambassadors, advocates, and even headhunters because they're armed with the same insight, messages, and stories that make them proud to be there, too.

But as you will soon discover, to successfully incorporate

the ideas presented in this book, you must be brave enough to swim against the tide. Why brave? Because the *give and get* isn't mainstream yet; most agencies are selling EVPs that lead with your strengths, benefits, and opportunities. The idea of articulating and openly embracing who should not apply is not the norm, so you must be "brave" enough to do something differently.

It means taking advantage of this approach before your competition does—before this becomes the norm. We believe it's about as brave as being the first woodcutter to use a chainsaw before all your ax-wielding competitors find out where to buy one.

We're not afraid of disrupting an industry because this isn't just a theory; it's a philosophy and methodology that has been tried and tested by some of the world's largest organizations to great effect.

Give and Get means leaning into the harsh realities of your organization, being open to proactively going out of your way to deter people from joining your organization, and even provoking some existing employees to rethink their career options.

We didn't write this book to just put the cat among the pigeons. We believe the traditional methodology is flawed for a variety of reasons that you will discover in the pages that follow. This book outlines a new, more human and effective way to brand and manage your employee experience to achieve excellence.

We want you to build an authentic, well-defined employer brand with employee propositions that contain deep resonance, that elicit powerful emotional responses as they speak to people on a level that no advertising slogan can achieve, because we address the derivative of what everyone ultimately cares and worries about, impact, purpose, and belonging.

Imagine an employer brand that's just refreshingly honest, simple, and clear—a brand that can inspire the best candidates to apply, despite the things that make it a hard place to work at times. Imagine an employer brand that also keeps your application volume manageable, because it can send someone running for the hills if they don't have what it takes to thrive within your culture.

If we can do that, when we look back we will be proud to have contributed to the journey we all find ourselves on together. That's our "Give" and our "Get," and we are grateful for your interest and support.

THE BIG
MISCONCEPTION

"The trouble with the world is not that people know too little;
it's that they know so many things that just aren't so."

—MARK TWAIN

Your EVP is designed to attract talent toward your organization. That's what the industry says. Google it, you'll find that basic premise all over the internet.

Yet, we believe the most valuable use of EVP is to help your organization *repel* talent.

As counterintuitive as it sounds, it's true. We want you to think of your employer and EVP as a smart filter that sits between your recruitment marketing and your recruitment, helping to weed out people who are unsuitable. For the good of the organization and for the good of those people, too.

The true value of EVP lies in articulating the expectations, harsh realities, vulnerabilities, and challenges people must be willing to overcome to thrive at your organization. Pair those with the benefits they stand to receive in return, and you'll be amazed what starts to happen to your recruiting funnel.

If you do it right, this will turn most people away. As crazy as that might sound, we believe it's essential to building a viable, productive, "happy" culture by design.

We believe in creating EVPs by using the premise that it's not a one-way broadcast of strengths, benefits, and opportunities but a value exchange that clearly articulates what a company wants, needs, expects, and demands in return for the spoils on offer. It's a two-way street. If you can communicate that message effectively by illustrating what it's really like, how someone is likely to feel, and what they must be prepared for on any given day, people are far more equipped to make an informed decision as to whether they have what it takes to thrive there and whether they want to take on the challenge.

For an organization that appreciates the value of happy, productive people to achieve business success, this approach is extremely valuable. The beauty of this is, 49 percent of candidates consciously cite knowing what it's really like to work somewhere as the number one obstacle to changing jobs. And 66 percent of candidates want to know about the culture and values most of all.

We call this mutual value exchange the *Give and the Get*.

It's important to articulate the *give* because it enables you to qualify applicants before they apply. Embracing the things that people need to be prepared to face, such as working lean or being ready to embrace a consensus-driven organization, enables you to repel anyone who isn't up for working that way.

If conventional employer brand is all about talent attraction, our methodology focuses on repelling the many to compel the few.

"Employer Brand 1.0 was all about talent attraction. We sold the hell out of Ping-Pong tables, happy hours, and bespoke coffee. The problem? It worked! We flooded our recruiting funnels with applicants seduced by our sizzle, overwhelming our recruiting engines and resulting in poor candidate experience and crushed hopes when our new hires joined and realized all the less exciting things we didn't share about the work environment.

"Fast forward to modern employer branding. We've learned from past failures and now realize that repelling the wrong talent is as important as attracting the right ones. We're getting better at telling authentic employee stories that capture the highs and lows of the job. Most importantly, we see our role as less 'hype man,' more conduit to creating more informed candidates."

—LARS SCHMIDT, FOUNDER OF AMPLIFY

When consulting with many different businesses of all shapes and sizes over the years, we've never worked with a business that just wants *more* applications. Everyone wants more of the *right* applicants based on competency, potential, culture alignment, and diversity.

If we stop thinking of an EVP as something to attract people to our brand and start thinking about it like a smart filter designed to reduce the number of applications, we can craft messages designed to help people self-select out who ultimately wouldn't be happy working at our organization.

After all, generating more applicants is easy. Give a half-competent marketing agency a few hundred dollars and access to your Facebook account and watch what happens, or read Bryan's first book, *Getting Goosebumps*, and make a plan.

However, before you do that, remember that unlike marketers, we can't sell to everyone. We reject 99 percent of the candidates who apply for every role, whereas our marketing counterparts would happily sell a product to anyone who agrees to pay for it. That makes the experience of applying for a job incredibly different from selling a product or service.

It also means that there is a lot more exposure to candidates leaving with a negative impression of our brand, and those experiences come at a cost.

WHAT IS THE HIDDEN COST OF DECLINED CANDIDATES?

Consider this: If your organization has 1,000 people and you turn over 15 percent each year, that's 150 open jobs. If you receive 100 applications for each open requisition, and each person has a social network of 500 people, your exposure is 7.5 million people. That 7.5 million people will form an impression of your organization based on what a rejected candidate has to say about their experience.

Seeing this simple math makes it startlingly clear that it's in our best interest to dissuade people from applying to our jobs if they:

- Have no chance in getting the job
- Would accept the role only to find the less-than-stellar parts of our environment that we neglected to mention and leave because they weren't prepared for it

Ninety-nine percent of the time, recruitment is in the rejection business, an appalling waste of time and money with significant human cost on both sides of the process. One of the most impactful ways to improve this situation is to use your employer brand and help more people self-select out of the process before they apply.

"In my experience, there are a few more skeptical audiences than job candidates, especially those in technical roles. At Job Portraits, we create content that speaks to the hard as well

as the exciting parts of a job. Candidates have told us over and over that what they really craved was more transparency about the hard times. Their question was never if things at their new job would get tough; they wanted to know what to expect when they did."

—MIKI JOHNSON, CO-FOUNDER OF JOB PORTRAITS

SUMMARY

We've never worked with a business that just wants *more* applications. Everyone wants more of the *right* applicants based on competency, potential, culture alignment, and diversity.

It's time to stop thinking of an EVP as something to attract people to our brand and start thinking about it like a smart filter designed to reduce the number of applications.

When you embrace the *Give and Get* philosophy, you'll likely find yourself in a conversation where you need to reiterate why it's in your best interest to trade in your braggadocio for humility. Here are a few reasons this method is so effective (credit to Job Portraits):

- **It's disarming.** If we feel we're being sold to, our mind shifts to defensiveness. Talking about what's not great about a job or who won't enjoy it causes candidates to drop their shields and get curious.

- **It builds trust.** Rather than coming off as overconfident or self-aggrandizing, you show candidates your team is open to constructive criticism and dedicated to continuous improvement.
- **It saves you time.** If your messaging brings in lots of candidates who aren't a good match, that's making your recruiting less effective. By being honest about a job's downsides, you give the wrong candidates a reason to self-select out, which reduces the noise in your funnel.
- **It draws in the right candidates.** Your business needs people who are excited to meet its biggest challenges. The sooner you surface those challenges, the more likely you are to find the candidates who see them as a fun problem to solve.

In the next chapter, we share one of our favorite examples of EVP embracing the *Give and Get* philosophy dating back hundreds of years, all the way to the French musketeers of 1618.

HOW DOES YOUR EVP COMPARE TO THE FRENCH MUSKETEERS OF 1618?

"All for one, one for all."

—*The Three Musketeers*

As an industry, employer branding is still in its infancy. Thought leaders are still pontificating over the correct terminology to use (employer brand vs. employment brand), conferences still have speakers teaching us "how to measure employer brand" and explaining the difference between employer brand and EVP. Many of the world's largest companies are only just now realizing the need for employer brand, or there's one lone "maverick" who got an internal promotion from a semi-related role and are left with a zero-dollar budget.

Despite how young the profession may seem, we can find examples of employer brand and EVP dating back hundreds of years, all the way to the French musketeers of 1618. In fact, it has been in effect ever since businesses formed, armies marched, and people had a need to band together and tackle adversity together.

In a meeting in 1618 between leaders of the Bohemian, Catholic, and protestant communities, a representative of the protestants read a letter affirming, *"As they also absolutely intended to proceed with the execution against us, we came to a unanimous agreement among ourselves that, regardless of any loss of life and limb, honor and property, we would stand firm, with all for one and one for all...nor would we be subservient, but rather we would loyally help and protect each other to the utmost, against all difficulties."*

This is the earliest known recording of the infamous phrase, *Un pour tous, tous pour un*, or as we all know it, *All for One and One for All*. That same phase later turned into the timeless literary classic, *The Three Musketeers*, written in 1844 by Alexandre Dumas.

Here's why *All for One and One for All* is so good and worthy of using as a benchmark for your EVP:

- It's concise and easily understood.
- It suggests the cultural values of the organization.
- It highlights a primary principle that's considered most important to everyone.

- It articulates the behavior you might expect to find.
- It clarifies both the promise to each individual and what contribution is expected from every individual too (the give and the get).
- Most of all, that simple phrase *All for One and One for All* contains a sense of purpose, impact, and belonging.

SUMMARY

If you audited your EVP, how many of those boxes would you check off? How does your EVP compare to the French musketeers of 1618?

In the next chapter, we'll take a step back and compare the traditional approach against the *Give and Get* framework. Looking at each framework side by side allows you to appreciate the differences, while also providing an understanding of how we got here as an industry and why it's time to evolve.

TRADITIONAL EMPLOYER BRAND FRAMEWORK VS. THE *GIVE AND GET* FRAMEWORK

―――

"Brand is just perception, and perception will match reality over time."

—ELON MUSK

If you compare the *Give and Get* framework to a traditional employer brand framework, a few things should jump out straight away:

- In the traditional model, the terms *brand essence* and *EVP* are often interchangeable.
- Rather than offering one EVP, we design one EVP for each employer brand pillar.

In the *Give and Get* framework, the EVP is never a slogan or a snapshot of an area of strength within the organization; we offer a clear value exchange that is taken from a common theme that can be found within the employee experience.

The traditional employer brand framework is deeply rooted in the traditional world of consumer branding. Simon Barrow, chairman of People in Business, and Tim Ambler, senior fellow of the London Business School first coined the phrase *employer brand* in the *Journal of Brand Management* in December 1996. This academic paper was the first published attempt to "test the application of brand management techniques to human resource management," and that's the direction the industry has taken ever since.

As the HR industry started to embrace employer branding, the term *employee value proposition* was born in the early 2000s. Brett Minchington was one of the first to offer a definition: "a set of associations and offerings provided by an organization in return for the skills, capabilities, and experiences an employee brings to the organization."

Conventional EVP does have a value exchange. The proposition is this: we want your skills, experience, and capabilities in return for a prescribed list of strengths, benefits, and opportunities we can offer you. It's transactional, but it's not a value exchange that fulfills or satisfies your talent audience.

The trouble is, it doesn't reveal anything about the employee experience. It doesn't answer the burning questions on the minds of candidates, and it doesn't acknowledge the sacrifice, commitment, and achievement of existing employees.

Coming from the origins of conventional brand thinking, is it any wonder, though? The value exchange of a customer is to purchase a product or service. Hopefully, a customer will "buy" into a brand in exchange for the transactional purchase price. If you're buying, we're selling, right?

Of course, while every prospective customer will be sold a product, no business on earth wants to hire everyone who steps forward.

The reputation of a company does not rest on how well a customer is able to use a product or service that you're selling. If you can't take a good photograph using an iPhone or if you don't make a very good cake after reading Gordon Ramsey's cookbook, most consumers don't blame the product; they accept their own culpability.

With employer brand, it's different. If you offer a poor candidate experience, or worse an experience that doesn't match your consumer experience, candidates blame you. On average, 249 people are turned away from every job vacancy in the United States. So it's important to remember that employer branding is closer to online dating than online selling.

That's the biggest reason why the traditional model isn't the perfect match when it comes to employer brand.

"It's in our DNA to want to be wanted by others. Knowing this gives talent acquisition a secret weapon. Where we fail is when we use our superpowers to attract everyone. We don't want to need everyone to apply to our jobs; we only want a few special candidates that will thrive within our culture. Ryan Reynolds in the movie Deadpool says, 'Your crazy matches my crazy, big time!' That is what we are talking about."

—TIM SACKETT

Traditional Model

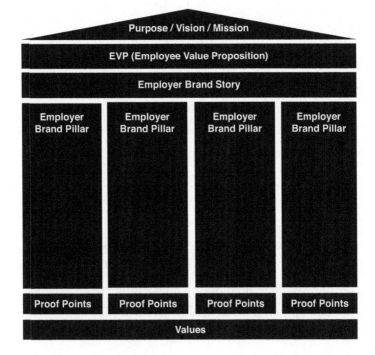

Give and Get Model

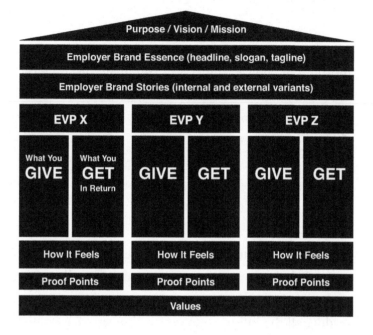

Purpose / Vision / Mission

Employer Brand Essence (headline, slogan, tagline)

Employer Brand Stories (internal and external variants)

EVP X		EVP Y		EVP Z	
What You **GIVE**	What You **GET** In Return	**GIVE**	**GET**	**GIVE**	**GET**
How It Feels		How It Feels		How It Feels	
Proof Points		Proof Points		Proof Points	
Values					

HOW TO CHANGE EMPLOYER BRAND AND EVP FOR THE BETTER

If you tell the truth about the positive aspects of a culture but leave out the harsh realities that may put people off from applying for a role at your organization, can you call that truly authentic?

We don't think anyone doubts an organization is telling the truth when they see employee success stories and positive descriptions about a workplace. But if we're honest, a lot of the time we also don't think it's the full story either, any more than we believe everyone's lives on Instagram are as good as they look.

It's inspirational and it's attractive to see strengths of culture, and of course, people want to know the employee experience can and will be positive and enjoyable. But more than anything, candidates crave more transparency about the hard times.

Which leads us to our next question: why did Glassdoor sell for $1billion?

Research shows that on average, a candidate will spend up to six hours researching a company before filling out an application. Why don't they just spend thirty minutes reading all the information on your careers website and then hit "Apply Now"?

Might it be that candidates don't believe everything they read on your careers website? Glassdoor, love it or hate it, provides an insight into what the employee experience is really like because it shares reviews left by real people working at the company.

Glassdoor doesn't always provide a balanced perspective; we often joke that it's what it's like to work at your company on your worst day. After all, if you're motivated to leave a review, it's usually amped up by significant positive sentiment or significant negative sentiment. Very rarely is someone motivated toward a review website to express a neutral opinion. However, in the absence of a well-rounded "truth" on your careers website, Glassdoor is a significant source of balance and insight into what could potentially lay ahead.

Comparably is a similar employee experience review site that is fast gaining ground on Glassdoor and shouldn't be ignored by any organization looking for ways to get a temperature check on the perception of their company culture and employee experience. At least this website's approach limits the anonymous feedback to valid employees, reducing the risk of misuse, and employee surveys and data they collect offer actual value to brands serious about striving to improve.

Only the organizations themselves are positioned with enough capacity to provide a fully rounded and balanced insight into what it's really like to work there.

What if we committed to providing all the answers necessary to satisfy the fundamental questions on a candidate's mind?

- What is it really like at your organization?
- Do I have what it takes to thrive at your organization?

The *Give and Get* employer brand framework is designed to help answer those burning questions. The construct and principles behind our framework help you effectively repel most of an external talent audience and compel the few, better-matched individuals to apply.

The key differences, of course, is that each employer brand pillar has an EVP, each one is made up of its own value exchange, defined by a *give* (what an employee must be prepared to provide, commit, or sacrifice) and a *get* (what an employee can expect in return).

The "how it feels" boxes are designed to help you describe the employee experience for each EVP on an emotional level using the most familiar and universally used language within the organization.

SUMMARY

It's time to rethink the way the industry approaches employer branding. This chapter makes it easy to see why a consumer marketing framework designed to sell a product to anyone who can afford to buy it is flawed when applied to selling jobs.

The *Give and Get* framework fills in the gaps to help you produce a mutual value exchange rather than a one-way broadcast of strengths.

It is our hope that the *Give and Get* framework is embraced by practitioners and agencies alike.

I (Charlotte) have built employer brands on both the traditional and *Give and Get* frameworks, and I have found the *Give and Get* to be far superior. Yes, it helped me repel the many and compel the few, but by having multiple EVPs it also gave me a crystal-clear roadmap of the types of stories I needed to tell my audience to show them what they would find behind the curtain. That piece was always missing from the traditional model, which may be why many of us have a hard time activating our employer brands.

Taking this a step further, next we want to show you how the *Give and Get* framework leans into and answers the burning questions that both candidates and employees are continually searching for.

In this next chapter, we will explore the essential ingredients needed to fulfill both sides of the value exchange from the perspective of how we're made to feel and what we must satisfy to be happy.

SOLVING FOR HAPPINESS

"Happiness is the consequence of personal effort. You must fight for it, strive for it, and insist upon it"

—REV RUN

At Ph., we lovingly call ourselves the "Defenders of Happiness." It sounds lofty because it is; it's an impossible idealistic pursuit. However, we're on a mission to continue to work with the world's biggest employers to help them articulate who they are and express their *Give and Get* such that people and companies can make better-informed decisions when it comes to where people work. We want a world where everyone loves their job. We know people search their entire lives for happiness, and our careers play a big contributing factor as to whether we find happiness. If we can help companies better articulate the true employee experience—the good, the bad, and the ugly—then candidates and hiring managers can make better-informed decisions to place people who can thrive, not just survive, in their position at work.

It's a known fact that we all spend more time at work with colleagues than we do at home with our family. You could argue that being happy at work is more than 50 percent of life's puzzle. Having been miserable in a job before leaving to start a business, Bryan can also attest to being unhappy at work doesn't stop at 5:00 p.m.; it of course spills into every aspect of our lives.

So when we talk about the focus of trying to "repel the many to compel the few," what we're really talking about is the outcome of having people better matched to jobs and careers where they will find more purpose, impact, and belonging. However, if we take that a step further, ultimately we want two things:

1. More effective and productive organizations to create a more cohesive and effective company culture.
2. More personal, individual fulfillment, which brings us the happiness we all want to get from our lives.

Companies always want to be more successful. And people just want to be happy. The (obvious) good news is, we can deliver company success by designing for happiness.

Looking at what intrinsically links these two things, it's the company culture. The culture is guided and defined by the employer brand, which is communicated using your employee value propositions.

If a company's value propositions work hard to better sign-post people toward an environment where they can shine and signpost them away from places they will not thrive at all, we've all got a much better chance of finding the success and happiness we're all searching for.

Happy people make a much more significant contribution to the success of a company. So we must solve for happiness.

What is happiness?

Big question, huh? There are quite a few different ways to answer, too. Happiness is essentially a positive experience of emotions. The emotions are made up of a cocktail of endorphins, dopamine, serotonin, and oxytocin, but that's just the science of how we process and assess happiness.

There have been several scientific studies to prove that happiness is a choice. The study published in 2013 in *The Journal of Positive Psychology* proved that if someone initially tries to be happier, they can become happier.[2] While that's great news, most of us do not consciously decide to be happy, and only 40 percent of our happiness is within our conscience control. We can safely assume that we are all a product of our environment—some people focus on

2   Yuna L. Ferguson and Kennon M. Sheldon, "Trying to Be Happier Really Can Work: Two Experimental Studies," *The Journal of Positive Psychology* 8, no. 1 (2013): 23. DOI: 10.1080/17439760.2012.747000.

and control those two elements more than others; some simply make decisions based on other conscious thinking.

The ancient Greeks believed that "happiness" was the joy we feel when striving after our potential. We love this because it implies happiness is intrinsically linked to life's purpose and the reason for being—something that directly supports the *Give and Get* methodology.

With all the testing, interviewing, questioning, listening, surveying, and observing of people we've done in the last fifteen years, we believe that there are several key ingredients that are always present when people tell us why they're happy at work.

The three primary ingredients (and two secondary factors) are:

1. A SENSE OF BELONGING

"Choose a job you love and never work a day in your life."

—CONFUCIUS

Feeling like you belong and have shared values, beliefs, and interests with others.

The mechanic of a *Give and Get* helps to provide a sense of belonging because it makes it easier to clearly showcase work ethic, personality, character, preferences, values, and behaviors of people, which in turn makes it easier for the talent audience to decide whether they identify with those people. If you use employee stories of challenge, achievement, progress, triumph, failure, motivation, and aspiration, you can allow your talent audience to live vicariously through the eyes of the employee and provide real insight into how it might feel to work at your organization, and in turn whether it's a place they could belong.

2. A SENSE OF PURPOSE

"It's not enough to have lived. We should be determined to have lived for something."

—WINSTON CHURCHILL

Feeling like you have something worthwhile to achieve, a reason you exist, and a goal to focus your attention and efforts toward that has personal meaning.

The mechanic of a *Give and Get* helps to provide a sense of purpose because it makes it easy to clearly articulate what's at the end of any struggle, challenge, or adversity. We answer the question of *why*. Why do people do what they do and what's possible if they do? If we're clear about what the company stands for and how that aligns with what everyone is working toward as a collective, it's easy then to demonstrate the meaning and the value behind the work.

3. A SENSE OF IMPACT

"Life is about making an impact, not making an income."

—KEVIN KRUSE

Feeling like you make a difference with what you do, a reason to keep doing what you're doing because you see the value you create and the difference you make.

The mechanic of a *Give and Get* helps to provide a sense of impact by default. If we consider the *Give and Get* as a simple input/output, we can illustrate what we must contribute to get the results. That can be articulated on any level, from executive vision down to grassroots, day-to-day work that is contributing toward the bigger picture.

There are two additional ingredients that admittedly can be found in the three above but are worthy of a special mention because they should be specifically accounted for when crafting an employer brand and EVPs.

4. A SENSE OF ACHIEVEMENT (TO BE DERIVED FROM PURPOSE + IMPACT)

"Comfort is the enemy of achievement."

—FARRAH GRAY

A feeling that validates your purpose and the satisfaction of making progress that satisfies your self-worth.

The mechanic of a *Give and Get* can help to provide a sense of achievement by either layering on messaging of how people feel when telling stories of impact and purpose, or simply by showcasing results and the evidence of progress, learning, and the journey leading up to the end results that provide the sense of achievement.

5. A SENSE OF FUN (TO BE DERIVED FROM PURPOSE, IMPACT, AND BELONGING)

"Don't take life too seriously; you'll never get out alive."

—ELBERT HUBBARD

You know: fun, enjoyment, smiles...maybe even the odd high five and occasional hug.

Demonstrating how and why your organization manages to put a smile on people's faces is incredibly important. Smiling, laughing, and having fun are all basic, fundamental validation that people can look to in order to imagine enjoying the employee experience. The power of a smile is not to be underestimated; it's a universal barometer of happiness and goes a long way to validate every aspect of your employer brand.

Laughter and smiles, even in stories of adversity, tragedy, and heartbreak, remind us we're all human; it helps us to empathize and reinforce the other aspects of our employer brand we want to communicate. Enjoyment is becoming an expectation, not a bonus. People want to know, *Can I be happy there?* Show them that they can, and give them the information to decide if your brand of happiness applies to them.

There are countless more ingredients to the happiness equation, but we've found these to be the main buckets.

If we organized more traditional considerations of an employee experience into the three main primary buckets, here's what it would look like:

1: BELONGING

Ethics, social conscience	Inclusion and diversity
Culture and values	Team and people
Working environment	Brand perception and reputation

2: IMPACT

Benefits and reward	Technology and resources
Compensation	Career mobility
Management and structure	Management and structure

3: PURPOSE

Mission and vision	Learning and development
Stability and consistency	Mentorship
Ethics, social conscience (again)	Innovation

Since 794 AD, in ancient Japan, the Japanese have used the word *Ikigai*, which roughly translated means *a reason for being, compassing a sense of joy, a sense of purpose and*

meaning and a feeling of well-being. The word derives from *Iki* meaning "life" and *kai* meaning the "realization of hopes and expectations." To achieve *Ikigai*, there are four principle questions you must be able to ask:

1. What do you love?
2. What are you good at?
3. What can you be paid for?
4. What does the world need?

When you look at our three primary buckets of impact, purpose, and belonging together with the secondary considerations of sense of achievement and fun, we believe there's a perfect alignment with *Ikigai*; however, these questions force us to think a little more specifically about the employee experience.

What's more, if we follow each question by asking *why*, we can start to add valuable context and correlate them even further.

Q: Why do you love what you do?

A: Because I find it fun, and I enjoy the challenge as well as the people I get to meet and collaborate with. I'm told I'm good at it, but I'm always having to learn, too. So the continual improvement and exploring new ways to achieve the result is just so attractive to me.

This sort of answer is something we hear quite a lot, and it's the perfect opportunity to further explore the specifics of what the real challenges are, how you've got to act with others, and what type of support makes the difference between continual learning and stagnating in a role. How does the struggle toward success and failure feel at your organization?

In short, with this approach you can start to quickly uncover your specific brand of purpose, impact, and belonging. You will hear evidence, examples, and stories of your specific brand of adversity, too. Each of these elements are essential to building a meaningful, unique, and effective *Give and Get*.

SUMMARY

With all the testing, interviewing, questioning, listening, surveying, and observing of people we've done in the last fifteen years, we believe these are the key ingredients that drive happiness at work:

1. A sense of belonging
2. A sense of purpose
3. A sense of impact
4. A sense of achievement derived from purpose and impact
5. A sense of fun derived from purpose and impact and belonging

Filling these buckets with the reality of your work experience is the key to being able to articulate what happiness looks like at your organization.

Next, we will examine a purpose-led company versus one's personal purpose. Both derive happiness but are often confused as one and the same. A beloved consumer brand is an attractive proposition, but it's not enough to win more than your fair share of top talent. It's the combination of being a purpose-led organization while relying on the personal purpose of your workforce that makes you stand head and shoulders above the rest. So let's look.

THE POWER OF PURPOSE-LED AND PERSONAL PURPOSE AT WORK

———

"Your identity is your most valuable possession. Protect it."

—ELASTIGIRL

We can remember several trends, hot topics, and subjects that have flowed in and out of popularity within HR since the early 2000s. From "Recruiters need to think more like marketers" to "There's a war for talent," there's always a headline *en vogue*. After those mantras came a focus on candidate experience (Ph.Creative may have had something to do with that one: see the reference to Virgin Media case study later in the book) followed by an industry obsession with storytelling.

We're privileged enough to observe trends and priorities firsthand from all the companies we visit, consult for, or advise. We're currently hearing two things everywhere we go.

The first is, "But we're actually a tech company now," which always raises a smile because despite it usually being semi-true, it's usually said as if it's a profound discovery that nobody else has thought of before. It's beautiful, though, because that very thought creates a mindset shift, a willingness to look at their market from a different perspective, which is essential to competing for the talent they require to move their organization forward.

The second is, "We're now a purpose-driven company," which is admirable, some would argue essential; however, it's no longer a unique point of difference. It's not enough to differentiate a company from talent competitors, and it's certainly not enough to win more than your fair share of top talent.

Let's shift gears. What is your favorite purpose-led company? There are a ton. They are inspiring, they give you goose bumps, and some even imprint on our own identity. We love Patagonia's ethics and commitment to sustainability and saving the planet. We admire Starbucks sourcing their coffee beans from ethical sources. We applaud airlines committed to making the world a smaller place by bringing families closer together to create the memories we'll cherish forever.

There are so many examples of purpose-led organizations that we could write a whole chapter showcasing the many ways organizations all over the world have gripped a sector, a nation, a generation, or a demographic because of what they believe and what they're trying to achieve.

But what exactly is a purpose-led company? A purpose-led company is an organization that is centered on one organized idea, which is engineered to improve the world and achieve something greater than financial gain. The existence and impact of the company has a strong moral stance, a view on the world that people can easily agree with and identify with.

Here's why it works: Organizations with an easily comprehensible purpose become instantly more memorable, relevant, and meaningful to us. As humans, we identify and form an affinity with the story we've experienced. Without a purpose, it's difficult to create an emotional connection. Unless there is an alternate compelling reason for us to admire the cool status of Levi's in the '80s, the novelty differentiation of Ben & Jerry's in the '90s, or the innovation of Apple reinventing the music industry.

We're all searching for our own purpose, and so as consumers, we align with the brands that reinforce the self-image we create for ourselves. If I buy only local, I'm supporting the community. If I buy organic, I'm saving the world from the negative effects of pesticides. If I buy from Tesla, I'm saving the environment from harmful emissions. If I buy the latest gadget, I'm a trendsetter.

Purpose-led brands make us feel good about our choices, which make us feel good about who we are. They help us construct or support a self-image and reinforce who we think we are or want to be.

If a purpose-led brand taps into an ideology that influences our actions, you could argue that the vision and purpose of a company is both critical and essential to building an organization that we all want to work for.

I (Bryan) have wanted to work with Nike ever since I watched *Back to the Future* with my dad in a cinema in Wales in 1985. I have no idea what Nike is like to work for, but if you're reading this, Nike, Marty McFly's Bruins had me at "Doc, Doc!"

I (Charlotte) have wanted to work with Lululemon ever since they emerged in 2000 and changed my work-from-home wardrobe forever. Although some appreciate the athleisure trend simply because they can wear yoga pants everywhere, Lululemon was originally created for people who led active lifestyles. For the founders, Lululemon was more than a place to buy activewear; they wanted to create a brand that could also serve as an avenue for people to meet others with common interests, learn about fitness and health, and feel comfortable and confident. It's like looking at someone on the street and saying, "You're wearing Lululemon. I'm wearing Lululemon. *Let's be besties.*"

Purpose-led brands like Nike and Lululemon have held a competitive advantage when it comes to talent attraction; however, a well-known consumer brand can be both a strength and a curse. Today, we would argue it's more a curse unless you have an appropriate employer brand and employee value exchange leading the charge.

The illusion of perception versus reality can be a challenging scenario when the employee experience fails to live up to expectations. Companies that have relied on the visibility and reach of their consumer brand to find talent often encounter problems such as limited diversity, high volume of mismatched applicants, and difficulties engaging top talent in the market.

Blizzard Entertainment is a classic example of an incredible company becoming a victim of its own success. The fan base and dedicated community of all of Blizzard games is staggering and stunning. It's unbelievable just how adored the Blizzard brand is because of the strength of their gaming community and how much it connects with the user base. Only until you've stood in an arena of twenty-five thousand fans, 95 percent of whom are dressed head to toe in Blizzard character costumes, chanting the names of sixteen gamers playing *Overwatch*, will you know what we mean when we try to articulate just how passionate this gaming community really is. It's breathtaking.

So much so that I (Bryan) have been walking around with Blizzard Entertainment Talent Acquisition (TA) Team members wearing Blizzard hoodies and T-shirts and witnessed people stopping them on the street like they're celebrities. TA has never been so popular, let me tell you. That said, Dina Medeiros, head of employer brand at Blizzard Entertainment, is one of my favorite humans of all time; she's at the top of her game, incredibly funny, and wicked-smart. However, it's not only her winning personality and employee brand strategy that's drawing the attention; it's a fan base clamoring to get an insight as to what it's like to work at Blizzard. They don't need more applications (they get a "Blizzard" of fans applying for every role); they need more of the right applications based on skillset and culture-add qualities.

A purpose-led company and a beloved consumer brand is an attractive proposition, a useful weapon to wield; it's expected to be there when we look for it, but it's not enough to win.

PERSONAL PURPOSE

From the day we start to consider what we want to be when we grow up or discover we have a talent, or even the day we have a strong opinion about something happening in the world or we find something rib-ticklingly funny, we start to build a picture of who we are and what we believe in. As we go through school or experience life, some of us are lucky enough to discover what we believe we're put on earth to do. Others spend their lives searching for something that provides fulfillment, purpose, and a sense of belonging.

For thousands of years, people much smarter than we are have written, experimented, and proved the innate human desire to find a sense of meaning in life.

Every one of us finds a way to answer that burning question—sometimes definitively, sometimes figuratively, and sometimes with a simple notion of finding satisfaction in the pursuit of progress toward something that feels positive, fulfilling, or worthwhile.

If we believe in something enough to want to effect change or to protect it so that it doesn't change, and you combine that belief with an ability to create impact, you could argue you've found your purpose in life. We may never achieve a result, but we take solace in knowing what we're "supposed" to work toward.

If we're good at something, we take satisfaction from doing it. If we're the best at something, we take pride in our achievements. If we're noticeably getting better at something, we take pride in our progress and stay focused on the future achievement we're working toward. This sense of pride feeds the soul.

We can agree with and be inspired by someone else's purpose, sure, but we feel emotionally fulfilled only when we demonstrate a sense of achievement toward our own purpose.

Over the course of the last few years, we've personally sat in more than 180 persona workshops listening to more than eighteen hundred people tell us about themselves. In these workshops, we listened closely for a variety of insights such as their motivators, drivers, priorities and preferences, values and behaviors. Above all, we listen out for what each person values and appreciates most in life. Armed with that information, we start to build a picture of how best to talk to them about what they care about in the language they can understand and positioned in a way that will get their attention and put them to the decision—is this a company I could work for?

"I send all of my voice-to-text messages with no corrections, no matter how bad the translation. I'm not sure how my friends feel when I tell them things like, 'You're the breast!' but it's added a lot of hilarity to my life.

"These technology blunders remind me that no matter how far we've come, we can't remove the human from Human Resources. The connecting of head and heart, the melding of passions and purpose—that will always be a human endeavor requiring the careful pairing of candidate needs and company offerings.

"We're all wired to do something that matters, but no one wants a one-size-fits-all job. We all want confirmation that we are uniquely suited for something significant. That's why attracting and keeping the right talent means helping them see the 'what's in it for me?' but also clearly articulating the WINFY: 'what I need from you' and why. And it must be authentic. The talent that stays in seat is the talent that finds resonance between their personal values and the role's purpose before day one."

—MICHAEL SMITH, WALMART

SUMMARY

A purpose-led company and a beloved consumer brand is an attractive proposition and a useful weapon to wield, but it's not enough to win more than your fair share of top talent. Don't forget to uncover the personal purpose of your workforce. It's the combination of being a purpose-led organization while relying on the personal purpose of your workforce that makes you stand head and shoulders above the rest.

In the next chapter, we'll explore what's possible when you combine a purpose-led company and personal purpose. We'll show you examples of brands that do this very well, as well as why it's so effective.

DO I HAVE WHAT IT TAKES TO BE A JEDI?

———

"True happiness...is not attained through self-gratification but through fidelity to a worthy purpose."

—HELEN KELLER

The oldest known story in the world was written sometime circa 1800 BC. Discovered in the ruins of an ancient library, the *Epic of Gilgamesh* was written across twelve clay tablets, depicting an adventure we've all heard before.

It's the story of a reluctant hero thrust toward a great adventure. Spurred on by a mentor, the hero is given some form of magic and is encouraged to live out their values in a decisive crisis, putting the hero to the ultimate test. Against all odds, the hero wins while facing their biggest fear. They return home transformed and help to restore order in the real world.

From Moses in the Bible to *Finding Nemo*.

From *The Matrix* to *Pretty Woman* and *Indiana Jones*.

From *The Lord of the Rings* and James Bond to *The Lion King* and *Batman.*

All these stories use the same formula—the hero's journey.

An anthropologist named Edward Burnett Tylor observed common patterns in story plots in 1871.[3] His work started more than a hundred years of study into "hero myth patterns," culminating in the world's most recognized mythologist, developing the well-known Joseph Campbell's *Hero's Journey.*

Campbell says we listen to these stories because they help us believe we can be heroes in our own lives. They help us remember that the most important thing in the world isn't getting rich or famous or finding a better mousetrap; it's making a difference in our communities and the world around us.

In other words, we're all searching for purpose and meaning. Ever since man was able to communicate, we have used the power of story to express the innate desire to belong.

Robert McKee, the world's foremost story expert, says that if the brain was hardware, the story would be the software we run to make sense of the world. Story is how we think,

---

3   Robert Segal, Lord Raglan, and Otto Rank, introduction to *In Quest of the Hero* (Princeton, NJ: Princeton University Press, 1990).

how we rationalize, memorize, and emotionally process everything that is happening around us.

For years, we've watched the label of "storytelling" rise through the ranks of populous marketing and communications, not because we're addicted to story, but because we're clinging to story as we search for meaning and purpose, more now than ever before.

Research shows that candidates today are attracted to purpose-driven brands up to 41 percent more than a company without a clearly defined purpose, but the story doesn't end there.

In the late '70s, George Lucas was struggling to make sense of a rehashed screenplay he was working on that was loosely based on *Flash Gordon* until one day he recruited the help of his friend Joseph Campbell.

Joseph Campbell applied his *Hero's Journey* story formula, and just a few short months later, *Star Wars* was born.

Do you remember the pivotal scene where Luke Skywalker is the final pilot to have a clear shot on the target to destroy the Death Star? As his hero's journey rushes toward a climactic end, his thumb hovers over the button before taking the final shot.

At that very moment, our hero Luke has two different kinds of motivation to hit that tiny target.

His external motivation is to destroy the Death Star and, in turn, save the galaxy from the perils of the empire.

At precisely the same moment, his internal motivation is to prove to himself that he has what it takes to become a Jedi like his father before him.

As candidates weigh up whether to pursue their next career move with your organization, they want to know that there are enough opportunities to progress. They also want to prove to themselves that they have what it takes to succeed.

Let us ask you a very important question: how can you start to imagine whether you have what it takes to succeed if you don't know what it takes to succeed?

The magic of using *Star Wars* to illustrate this point is the genius of the story architecture that combines the personal purpose of the hero with the professional purpose of a company that the hero aligned to.

We've come up with a simple formula to demonstrate this idea.

INWARD MOTIVATION		OUTWARD MOTIVATION		LUKE'S RESULT
Personal purpose	+	Corporate purpose that I buy into	=	Complete alignment
Do I have what it takes to become a Jedi?	+	Do I want to defeat the empire and save the universe	=	My life has meaning, purpose, and impact. I'm where I'm meant to be, doing what I'm meant to be doing.

The outward motivation represents the rational wants, the benefits, and opportunities our hero can expect to encounter.

The inward motivation represents the emotional needs of our hero, both of which are incredibly important for different reasons.

HOW TO ALIGN PERSONAL PURPOSE WITH AN ORGANIZATION

A purpose-driven employer brand like Nike or Lululemon inspires us to lean in. They gain our attention based on communicating core values that resonate with our values and they share messages that create affinity. And when brands layer on the use of an EVP to convey their strengths, benefits, and opportunities, they start to answer most of a candidate's external motivations.

But there are vital pieces missing from almost all the EVPs in use today.

Without understanding the adversity before us, the size of the challenge we face, and the impact we can make, we can't possibly start to quantify how our own personal purpose aligns with an organization, however aspirational and inspirational the corporate vision and employer brand positioning.

We all want to know: do we have what it takes to become a Jedi at your organization?

For every individual career path in every single business, the answer to that question is often *no*. If that wasn't the case, everyone would be in their perfect job with 100 percent levels of satisfaction and fulfillment.

We owe it to our audience to make it easier to decide. We owe it to our recruiters to be able to identify what our brand of Jedi looks like and how to let them know we think they belong with us.

We owe it to all concerned to tell the whole story, which is more of a value exchange than a broadcast of strengths benefits and opportunities.

Employer brand and EVP isn't marketing to a talent audience. If it was, we'd hire everyone we attracted to apply. It's having the confidence and conviction to polarize and crystallize who we are and then having the clarity and self-awareness to articulate why people should care and what it takes to find meaning and purpose within.

"Today there is more information available for candidates to consume than at any point in modern history. This information includes career sites, review forums, social media and so much more. It is absolutely driving sentiment and action of the job seekers as much as Amazon reviews and commercials are driving consumer behaviors and purchase decisions. On top of this, there is a tidal wave of content bombarding the candidate. Company after company shouting as loud as they can about their culture, openings and benefits. It can be both empowering and overwhelming to a job seeker.

"In the age of buzzword bingo (Innovate! Disrupt! AI! Bring Your Whole Self to Work!) and content overload, the real effective employer brands are less and less prevalent. Most companies want to take the 'we are universally loved' market position, but human DNA does not operate that way. The best employer brands are the ones that take chances and are who they are in a public (and human) way. If you don't like what you see, sorry. If you do, you will love working here. This is what creates fans of any product or company. Vanilla is an awesome ice cream flavor, but in marketing it does zero. It doesn't attract, it doesn't repel, it just is."

—ED NATHANSON, FOUNDER OF RED PILL TALENT

SUMMARY

Luke ultimately decided to embark on his hero's journey not because it was going to be easy or because he blindly wanted to claim Jedi status. He was all-in because of the trials and tribulations he knew he had to face to complete his personal transformation. Obi-Wan made it clear just how difficult the road ahead was. It was the very nature of the challenge and adversity that made the purpose so meaningful to Luke.

The result was that Luke was suitably motivated by the alignment of both external and internal motivations, with a sense of belonging and shared purpose.

The principles of *Give and Get* are focused toward being able to answer the burning question, "Do I have what it takes to be a Jedi?"

Now that you are comfortable with the mindset of your candidates and how to best motivate someone with a *Give and Get*, let's shift gears and learn how to produce an equally balanced *Give and Get*.

BUILDING AN EMPLOYER BRAND AND EVP WITH THE *GIVE AND GET*

"Unless both sides win, no agreement can be permanent."

—JIMMY CARTER

To create a useful *Give and Get* that will quickly help a candidate self-select in or out, help a recruiter spot an ideal candidate, or remind a great employee why they're already working for you, it's important to understand the approach behind how to produce an equally balanced *Give and Get*.

Crafting a Give and a Get is more valuable than matching a pro with a con. Unfortunately, saying something like, "There's no work-life balance here, but the bagels are great," isn't what we're striving for.

The principle of a strong *Give and Get* is based around showcasing strengths, benefits, and opportunities within the context of what it takes to truly thrive and capitalize on what's on offer at your organization. In other words, if there's something your people really desire, appreciate, or believe in, the *Give and Get* proposition spells out what it takes to achieve it by leaning into the main universal drivers of impact, purpose, and belonging.

The theory is simple at its core. Answer the questions surrounding *"Do I have what it takes to be a Jedi?"* that we explored in the previous chapter.

Before crafting a *Give and Get*, you must be clear on the different ingredients that can reflect the realities of your employee experience that also contribute toward purpose, impact, and belonging. The five ingredients are:

1. Vulnerabilities of the organization
2. Harsh realities of the organization
3. True behaviors found throughout the organization
4. Strengths and benefits that make a difference to the employee experience
5. Opportunities appreciated throughout the employee experience

Before we dive deeper into each ingredient, let's review a typical example that illustrates each category in the form of an employee experience narrative. Ph.Creative summarizes insights in this way to position the ingredients and balance the Gives and the Gets.

EMPLOYEE EXPERIENCE NARRATIVE

Vulnerability. We're a market leader; however, we're unusually behind the curve in several areas when it comes to our competition, so it's essential to the business that we close the gap. When we release our tech this year, it's got to be received well, and as it stands, we need more expertise in certain areas to make sure that happens.

Harsh realities. We're under incredible pressure to maintain an annual software release cadence, which means there's never much work-life balance, and the demands you get from your team create pressure that you feel all year round. It's unrelenting.

Our audience can be hypercritical, and the expectations to drive the market forward can be overbearing and overwhelming at times.

Secrecy and information sharing can take a bit of getting used to here. If you don't need to know something, you will not be given any information at all. If you do need something to help with your work, you're given and expected to know everything.

The organization runs lean, and quite often there's a lack of enough resources to get something done comfortably. You must think creatively, work together as a close team, and apply brute force and just put the hours in to get things done.

If you don't carefully manage your time, it's easy to burn out quickly, and there's not much help or support around you to avoid it. The more you give, the more you give.

True behaviors. Everyone around you is super "to the point"; they demand your best work all the time and can be short with you if you don't explain yourself well and quickly. If you don't take the time to get to know someone, they won't answer your email, never mind stop to help you with something. Incompetence is never tolerated by anyone; lazy efforts are exposed by everyone.

If you're in uncharted territory with your work and need guidance or input ahead of a breakthrough, your peers will dial in and help quickly. Often, if your problem risks the progress of a project, you can find yourself surrounded by incredibly smart experts willing to selflessly collaborate without a second thought or any judgment at all. Once the challenge is overcome, there's no ego, no big thanks parade needed; life just carries on as usual.

Relevant strength. There is a commitment to world-class quality, and so you will never be questioned for making a decision that maintains the brand standard if it's clear you've acted with integrity. You will never be asked to cut corners or compromise your work for a deadline.

The scale of your team means there's always somewhere to turn for niche expertise of the highest order. The diversity of your team means there's always someone who will look at your challenge from a different perspective, so it's easy to get creative, think differently, and try new ways to overcome any challenge that presents itself.

There's a good chance you will see the product of your own work in the hands of millions of people every day.

Opportunities. You learn here faster than anywhere else in the world by the very nature of the environment. It's fast paced, and there's excellence and cutting-edge developments all around you. Your leadership team will knock down walls to help you get where you need to be because they've been in your shoes and they understand what you're going through.

If you love what you do, you'll get the chance to indulge that passion to the limits and find out what you are capable of, backed by a company that cares about making the world a better place.

You will soon be pushed to become the very best version of yourself, and it's very possible you will be capable of and responsible for something that amazes even yourself once you're done.

As a recognized pioneer brand, it is comforting to know we're one of the good guys. Here, you get the opportunity to do your best work with a clean conscience and strive to protect people's rights, their privacy, and freedom.

After you've proven yourself here, it's easy to move through the ranks quickly, and there's not another company that wouldn't hire you after working here. For global recognition and reputation, it doesn't get better.

After reading this narrative, it's easy to spot some obvious Gives and Gets.

If you'd like to test yourself further, below are four fictional employer brand pillars. See if you can finish each statement using the information presented in the narrative. If you skipped the last chapter, go back and read it now so that the *Ikigai* reference below makes sense.

COMPLETE COMMITMENT (*IKIGAI* PURPOSE)

You must be capable and willing to **Give**: _____

As a result, you can expect to **Get**: _____

ONLY THE BEST RESULTS (*IKIGAI* PROFESSION)

You must be capable and willing to **Give**: _____

As a result, you can expect to **Get**: _____

ALWAYS INDEPENDENT THINKING (*IKIGAI* PURSUIT)

You must be capable and willing to **Give**: _____

As a result, you can expect to **Get**: _____

TEAM COMES FIRST (*IKIGAI* PASSION)

You must be capable and willing to **Give:** _____

As a result, you can expect to **Get:** _____

VULNERABILITIES

"What makes you vulnerable makes you beautiful."

—BRENÉ BROWN

People are drawn to authenticity and truth. It's endearing when people use self-deprecating humor. It's refreshing when someone admits a weakness. It's compelling when you're asked for your help because one of your strengths is recognized and appreciated.

Most of all, when you're vulnerable, you imply honesty, which is what builds trust, affinity, and real engagement.

Blake Snyder, the Hollywood screenwriter and author, calls it the *save the cat* moment. In many movies of note, the protagonist will do something early on to create empathy with the audience. Even if the lead character is a tough guy or an evil genius, Hollywood will have them do *something* that demonstrates a redeeming feature of their character. When we see that act, it allows us to relate with them sufficiently such that we can root for the hero all the way through the movie.

In *Serpico* (classic 1973 movie), Al Pacino plays a tough-guy cop character who is so mean, it's hard to like him. His goal is to catch a group of criminals, so he engineered a fake competition and informed all the criminals that they had won a private meet-and-greet tour of Yankee Stadium. It worked, and all but one of the bad guys turned up and got caught.

The one remaining criminal eventually turned the street corner just as the others had been read their rights and carted off to jail. It wasn't too late to catch him. However, he had brought along his son to meet the baseball stars.

Al Pacino's character could have disregarded the son; however, in a split-second, you see him quickly flash his badge and warn off the criminal dad as he says, "Sorry, the tour is canceled for today," letting the man known to get his son out of there. As the man nodded his appreciation and quickly turned on his heels, Al Pacino shouts, "Catch you later."

His *save the cat* moment was compassion for the dad; he didn't want his son to witness his dad getting arrested. In that moment of great empathy, the audience sees there's a caring side to him and warms to the character from that moment on.

You could interpret Al Pacino's actions as being a weakness;

after all, he failed to catch the criminals. But if you've got a beating heart in your chest, you physically feel the empathy on display. His actions bring you (the audience) closer to him, and the same can be said for any organization that chooses to *save a cat* or demonstrate a vulnerability.

If you have not read *Dare to Lead*, we highly recommend it. Brené Brown talks about the benefit of owning your vulnerabilities and eloquently positions the idea of vulnerability as a strength—in fact, more than that, the derivative of love, belonging, joy, courage, empathy, and creativity.

Being vulnerable is not something we see much of every day, but it doesn't take a huge stretch of the imagination to see that if you dare to be more open and honest about your whole self, it's a powerful way to let people in—to connect with you on a deeper level.

Imagine organizations had the same amount of courage to be vulnerable. To admit the gaps. To talk about the challenges, the adversity, and the long road ahead. What's the worst that could happen? People find out you're not perfect. Statistically speaking, people don't trust brands. No company on earth is perfect. The upside is, if you admit your imperfections, the vision yet to be realized is the biggest opportunity to engage, motivate, and connect with people. If you back up a vulnerability with the conviction to change, improve, or do good, it can be incredibly alluring and very difficult to resist, especially when you believe you could have a significant role in getting them there.

Talking about a vulnerability doesn't mean talking about something that's particularly negative or a major disadvantage to competition.

Knowledge gaps, technology gaps, resource gaps in comparison to industry standard, competitors, or basic expectations are typical examples of a harsh reality people want to know before joining a company. To some, having a base level of technology at a place of work is a must-have. To others, having existing expertise in a team is essential. And for others, the very idea that these gaps exist is appealing because people can see a gap they can fill. For some, we've just illustrated a clear place for the right person to come in and add value, create impact, and feel valued.

HARSH REALITIES

"Nobody is going to hit as hard as life, but it ain't how hard you can hit. It's how hard you can get hit and keep moving forward."

—ROCKY BALBOA

Have you ever seen the movie *The Invention of Lying* with Ricky Gervais? It's what we'd call a good little Sunday afternoon movie. The basic premise is that nobody in the world ever lies until one day, Ricky Gervais's character finds himself telling a lie to make his dying mother feel better about passing away. From a position of pure compassion, he confidently tells his mother there is a god and there is a heaven, and at that moment she is flooded with warmth and happiness as she passes away. The trouble is, someone overhears his lie, and the world begins to spiral out of control as a result.

Up until then, Ricky Gervais paints a hilarious picture of what the world would be like if everyone just told the truth.

Being the employer brand geeks that we are, we started to imagine what job descriptions would be like in this world. Can you imagine?

Data entry executive wanted:

Someone to turn up every day without fail and sit in a drab cubicle and enter as much inane information into a spreadsheet as humanly possible.

The role seemingly makes no difference to anyone's life, but the company does require the data to be transferred from paper to digital format to reduce space in the office, risk of fire, and loss of historic communications. To get through the day, you need to be mentally resilient and willing to work alone for long periods.

Unless you can zone out, multitask, or focus on a greater goal you're working toward while using this job for the money, most people can do this work for only about five months before leaving due to incredible boredom and/or a deep sense of soul-destroying worthlessness that sometimes also leads to clinical depression. However, if you demonstrate a willingness and the capability to do these low-level and mundane tasks for more than six months, there is a significant opportunity to stand out as someone worthy of more responsibility and interesting work, which follows quickly from that point.

The dress code is annoyingly strict, especially because you don't see many people all day; however, it does mean you can watch TV or listen to podcasts while doing your job, and there is free coffee to keep you awake and alert. The kitchen is subsidized, so it's cheap, which means it's easy to meet lots of new people.

The pay is above average due to the mind-numbing routine, and if you stay longer than twelve months, there is a sizable bonus. There are several great outdoor activities close by, and it's not uncommon for people to start early to get out the door at 3:00 p.m. every day and enjoy the afternoons in the sun.

A big perk of the job is that you can have a large amount of training paid for by the company, so a lot of people use this role as a stepping stone to qualify for a much more interesting job either here or even somewhere else; plus, while you're doing training, you're not having to do the role you're being paid for, so that's good, too.

We would like applicants to have a degree of some sort; however, it's such a difficult role to fill, the chances are, we'll take anyone who can demonstrate basic typing and literacy skills. So please be as thorough with any other experience or evidence of resilience and staying power as you can.

If you're willing to risk your sanity in the short term in return for above-average remuneration and the flexibility to do more interesting things in life, apply now.

Obviously, this role sounds horrendous, but the applicants know exactly what they're getting themselves into. The sheer honesty of the description gives the audience a sense that they can trust it's a balanced insight into what it's really like—there's no hidden downside to this role; it's all up front.

Anyone applying for this role after reading this description has already mentally prepared to endure the hardships, they have decided they can stick it out, they've assessed the upside and decided it's worth it. Anyone applying for this role is now culturally worth talking to.

Maybe this job description takes the point way too far, but

we couldn't resist thinking about how simple life would be if we all took this approach. The reality is, there are so many jobs that would appeal to a large audience even if the harsh realities were front and center.

In our experience, employees are far more likely to willingly contribute toward advocacy efforts if it feels authentic and balanced, instead of being asked to "sell" why it's such a great place to work.

Advocacy increases when you apply the *Give and Get* because employees start to wear harsh realities like a badge of honor. They galvanize your internal audience because when they read the stories you're producing, they empathize with how it *feels* to work there.

We've all seen those videos of smiles, high fives, and cringingly bad messages of "It's awesome here every day" and nobody believes them for a second. Instead, we shoot straight over to Glassdoor to dig into what's really going on.

FIVE REASONS *NOT* TO JOIN YOUR ORGANIZATION

If it was your job to persuade people not to join the company and you couldn't lie, what would you say?

This is one of our favorite questions to ask when researching an employer brand or introducing the concept of *Give and Get* on stage at a conference. Usually, it takes a little bit of warming up to, but once you get a room talking, they always know the answers and it can be super-therapeutic, too.

FIVE REASONS NOT TO JOIN PH.CREATIVE:

Our salaries and benefits are not always as competitive as the big corporate competitors. When you're a giant killer, you often can't compete with brute force. So if your number one priority is money, we're probably not the agency for you.

Everyone in the entire business is required to be comfortable making decisions, being accountable, and taking assertive action. If you're not a confident person and you prefer more comfort, infrastructure, and process around you, you will struggle to perform well in our team. Agency life requires quick thinking, problem solving, and urgency. At Ph., this is very true, and if you're not comfortable working at pace with continual consequences, if you slow down and cause delays to clients or teammates, you will not enjoy your experience here.

At Ph.Creative, we trust people to use common sense, and there is a lack of process in many areas of the business that instead relies on making sound choices yourself based on situations that present themselves. If you can't cope with operating in the gray, Ph.Creative will drive you crazy.

Being a very creative, driven organization, it's not uncommon to find decisions and minds being changed on projects, strategy, and client work in favor of new ideas, better solutions, and even gut feel or just dissatisfaction with how something is turning out. Chopping and changing from time to time can frustrate the life out of people who prefer a long and clear runway of what's expected and what's required to finish something start to finish.

Star performers can easily become overburdened with work because everyone loves working with the best talent in the agency. If you're a people pleaser, if you love your work, and you know you could do a great job, it can be super tough to resist taking on extra work. The net result is that people can get burned out if they're not realistic with their own workload.

Imagine all recruiters were equipped with a "Top five reasons to join" your organization cheat sheet. Now, after every top reason, you had a caveat that warned people against something they must be willing to put up with or cope with to realize each benefit.

"Attract the best, deflect the rest."

—BARI POLAY, TALENT BRAND MANAGER, LYFT

Think of the consistency and continuity you're creating in your team, but now also imagine the candidate's reaction.

Even if they decline, they respect you for telling the truth, and you've just saved yourself the expense of putting them forward. If they progress, they're armed with the truth and ready to tackle it, too.

You may be asking yourself, "What are the risks of being up front about the less desirable sides of your company?"

We think it's the wrong question.

We (talent audience) know flaws, weaknesses, and harsh realities exist in every business. We just don't know what they are right away...until we read the plethora of company review websites.

We're in a world where it's no longer possible to control your brand. The best you can do is influence it. What better way to influence your brand reputation than with the truth?

Incidentally, harsh realities come and go. Things changes. That's why your employer brand should stand the test of time, but your EVP is like a florist's shop window; it must be sense checked annually.

CHALLENGING AND SUPPORTING BEHAVIORS

"I'm selfish, impatient and a little insecure. I make mistakes, I

am out of control and at times hard to handle. But if you can't
handle me at my worst, then you sure as hell don't deserve me
at my best."

—MARILYN MONROE

Culture can be defined as nothing more than a set of consistent behaviors found within an organization. We like this definition because it's simple. The reason someone wants to know about the culture of a company is that they want to assess whether they are a good match. If we do a good job of accurately describing the typical behaviors that people consistently exhibit within a company, we're providing a valuable, useful service to our audience.

Candidates want to know if they could feel like they belong. There's a subtle difference between the two. The challenge we have with how culture is positioned in most employer brands is it's usually presented as a benefit and celebrated as something people are lucky to be part of when in fact it's more of a question of whether there is a good match or not. Even the most celebrated or renowned working cultures in the world aren't for everyone, and it's not good enough to simply claim, "We have a great culture"; it must be justified with evidence, tangible examples. And quite frankly, your own opinion of *good* or *bad* is irrelevant; it's for the employees and candidates to decide for themselves. Our job is to equip them with all the necessary information to make an informed and correct decision based on what they see and who they are.

A typical means of articulating culture is talking about the values of an organization.

Obviously, the shared values of an organization drive the behaviors you will find within an organization, so it's a logical place to start. However, values alone are not enough to accurately set expectations of how it might feel to work in your company because values are open to interpretation, they are intangible, and they're always positive.

Have you ever seen a company that publishes values such as, "Lazy," "Arrogant," or "Combative"? If you do ever see this, please email us because we would love to see it.

So we're back in the land of "Integrity," "Honesty," and "Fun." But what does "fun" really mean? If you think about it, it's as good as useless when trying to articulate an employee experience because your idea of fun might be completely different from mine.

So how does talking about challenging and supporting behaviors help to better describe how it might feel to work at your company?

CHALLENGING BEHAVIOR EXAMPLES:

"If you ask a colleague for help before getting to know them first, there's a good chance you could be flat-out ignored here."

"If you take too long to get to the point when communicating to people here, you'll find everyone will quickly lose patience with you because the environment is extremely fast paced and to the point."

"There's a consistent expectation of doing work to an incredibly high standard, which means there's always an above-average level of work-related pressure and even stress you just have to deal with on any given day."

SUPPORTING BEHAVIOR EXAMPLES:

"Everyone has a little bit of geek in them here. Doesn't matter what it is, but you'll quickly find that most people obsess over something they're passionate about, and if you're willing to share your passion, people will love listening about, learning about who you are and what makes you tick."

"If you have a personal issue, challenge, or problem, you'll immediately get instant support from everyone around you. We put family first every time when it matters most."

THE POWER OF COMBINING THE TWO TYPES OF BEHAVIORS TOGETHER

Quite often, talking about both supporting and challenging behaviors in one story is a great opportunity to present your audience with an easy choice to make using cause and effect:

> "At Ph.Creative, if you're seen to be working super-hard on a project, but you're still falling behind with a deadline because of the sheer volume of work, there's a very good chance your teammates will rally round and put some extra hours in to help you. However, if you're the type of person to clock watch and do the bare minimum, when you're under pressure to deliver to a tight deadline, or you need help from your teammates to get something done, most likely you'll have to deal with it yourself. Showing a willingness to hustle and support your teammates is one of the best ways to earn respect at this company, which seems to be incredibly important to the vast majority of us here."

The example above paints a clear picture of both supporting and challenging behaviors, but it also tells a relatable story and allows the audience to make an educated and informed self-assessment and subsequent decision as to whether they could feel like they belong in a given culture.

Am I the clock watcher or the team player? Would feeling

the support of a team around me when it really counts matter to me?

If we combine any of the supporting and challenging behaviors from the lists above, watch how the balanced view starts to become more authentic, believable, and valuable to your audience.

COMBINING BEHAVIORS TO CREATE MORE CONTEXT AND BALANCE

Let's look at how we might combine these behaviors to create a statement that reflects the principles of a strong *Give and Get*.

Challenging Behavior

> "There's a consistent expectation of doing work to an incredibly high standard, which means there's always an above-average level of work-related pressure and even stress you just have to deal with on any given day."

Supporting Behavior

> "If you have a personal issue, challenge, or problem, you'll immediately get instant support from everyone around you, and work priorities are simply discarded. We put family first every time when it matters most."

What we've managed here is to create a scenario that:

- Existing employees agree with wholeheartedly
- Existing employees will be proud and appreciative of to the point where they will be willing to share and advocate
- Candidates will appreciate and believe to be authentic
- Candidates will be able to make an accurate decision as to whether they want to be part of that culture
- Is easy to find real human stories to back up your claims, which means activating your EVP gets infinitely easier and incredibly more powerful

When you compare this approach to the typical aspirational or just one-sided positive narrative, you typically find within an EVP there's no comparison.

WHY THIS WORKS SO WELL

Typically, the challenging behaviors come from the pressure of the business strategy and leadership. The supporting behaviors come from the employees and leadership in response to the pressures of the business strategy and leadership. This means the net result is a clear insight into what it really takes to thrive, not just survive.

STRENGTHS AND BENEFITS THAT MAKE A DIFFERENCE TO THE EMPLOYEE EXPERIENCE

"Pleasure in the job puts perfection in the work."

—ARISTOTLE

At last, we get to talk about how good we are! Ha, of course it's OK to talk about the strengths and benefits of an organization; it can't all be downside!

The good news is that with the *Give and Get*, your audience is more receptive and trusting of a company talking about genuine strengths and valuable benefits. In fact, once a candidate has digested the adversity of a working environment, the bounty can quickly become sweeter.

The key to harnessing the value of strength within an organization is identifying the tangible benefits to the employees and their working experience, as well as being able to identify what matters most universally and individually at a personal level.

EXAMPLES OF STRENGTHS

The financial strength of an organization is not a strength in isolation. If the finance offers stability, extra resources, sizable pension contributions, or a significant continual learning program that is highly desirable to employees, then it becomes a strength that is highly relevant and a valuable ingredient to the *Give and Get* of your EVP.

Having an organization filled with some of the world's top experts in their field is an incredible strength if you're trying to cure cancer. The benefits of that company's strength to an employee can vary from a belief that they can really change the world, or it could be the fact that they would have access to learn from incredibly smart experts.

It's our job to effectively illustrate the strengths and benefits, and there are some fundamental questions our talent audience needs to address.

ARE THE BENEFITS WORTH THE SACRIFICE?

If the benefits don't measure up to the adversity people are willing to face, then Houston, we have a problem.

Just like with our core values, talking about the strengths of an organization in isolation doesn't necessarily offer up the full picture to a candidate or any significant insight either. In fact, positioned incorrectly, strength might be perceived as negative if it means there's little room for someone to come in and make an impact.

For example, a software engineer who loves to build things from scratch might be put off finding that the team is already incredible, the systems are awesome, and there's not a lot of new ground required to cover. Identifying the most prevalent accompanying benefits that follow on from that company strength is the only way to ensure you're creating a value exchange that your talent audience cares about and values.

WHAT'S MORE INTERESTING THAN LEARNING ABOUT COMPANY STRENGTH?

Learning the story of how a strength became a strength. People are attracted to the current state especially if they've bought into how and why you arrived there. Coupled with the future, the strengths of your organization can become irresistible to the right person.

Opportunities

Opportunities within an organization come in all shapes and sizes. As you have read through the ingredients, thinking about your harsh realities or challenging behaviors, you probably also considered the upside to be able to cope, operate, or even thrive in those conditions; each one has a natural opportunity attached to it.

The opportunities you find will be specific to your organization. Some will have been clearly defined and designed as part of career development. Some opportunities exist due to unique circumstances, such as working for an airline that might present the opportunity to travel anywhere in the world for free on your days off.

Examples of Opportunities

- Working for an organization that allows you to help local communities or support your favorite charity.
- Working for a TV streaming company might mean you get a free monthly subscription for you and your family—watching *Game of Thrones* as much as you want might be a big deal to a lot of people!

It's important to have a good handle on all the natural upside to working at your organization and how much people value and appreciate them. You will discover other opportunities as part of your employer brand research. These hidden or previously unknown opportunities can be the key to creating meaningful, impactful EVPs that will help you repel and compel at will.

SUMMARY

In summary, just remember in vulnerability there is an opportunity to discover, explore, grow, learn, excel, advance, develop, create, or contribute.

In strength or advantage, there are opportunities to invest, learn, accelerate, progress, or earn.

In harsh realities, there are opportunities to cope, learn, thrive, prove yourself, develop, change, disrupt, and champion.

Only by digging into the full challenging side of your employee experience can you discover the universal drivers and motivators that keep people coming back. Sometimes these insights can be surprising; they can be seemingly small and insignificant. However, herein lies the super-powers to your EVP.

Now that you know how to produce a meaningful *Give and Get*, let's turn our attention to the research phase and focus in on how to find the truth within your organization.

CATCHING TRUTH

"Research is to see what everybody else has seen and to think what nobody else has thought."

—ALBERT SZENT-GYÖRGYI

Over the years, we've honed a variety of questions designed to solicit the truth from people. Sometimes we ask the same question many times in different ways; sometimes we have people draw their answers, act them out, video their experiences, relay stories, or even show us examples of what they do.

If you remember only one thing from this chapter, let it be this: *extracting the truth from someone isn't as easy as just asking.*

Over the years, we've concluded that merely asking, listening, and documenting answers isn't enough to get to the truth. There's an art and science to it. Discovering the truth requires asking insightful questions, then listening to answers, followed by empathetic dialogue to discover their real point of view.

That said, this chapter may be the most valuable lesson in the book because we share the tactics we've honed over the years to help you catch the truth within your organization. Having worked with many agencies over the years, I (Charlotte) have never seen an agency as good on their feet as Ph.Creative. I learned more from working with them than any other agency I've had the privilege to work with.

ASKING AND LISTENING ISN'T ENOUGH

"Never miss a good chance to shut up."

—WILL ROGERS

Does this sound familiar?

You: "Hey, how are you?"

Best friend: "I'm fine, thanks."

You: "Really? You don't look fine. What's really going on?"

Best friend: "Is it that obvious? OK, so…"

Imagine what sort of friend you would be if you only ever took the first answer as the truth? Go deeper than answers you get on the surface.

When you do this, you start to find patterns, correlations,

and common themes, yet discrepancy and incongruences, all of which become a myriad of different "truths."

It is these truths that provide the foundation for building something unique that can't be replicated or copied. Instead, it can be used to remind people why they do what they do with such passion, or to find people who are perfect additions to a given culture—possibly even find their true calling.

You can't find that level of insight with a survey. Dave Hazlehurst at Ph.Creative always says, "Data tells us what; people tell us why," which is such an insightful reminder that surface answers just aren't good enough and usually the pure gold is waiting just beneath the surface.

Quite often, we find lots of commonality on the surface. And while that's a good thing, it's not enough insight to build something special. For example, say your quantitative results reveal "43 percent of people are passionate" or "62 percent are proud to work here." Resist the urge to lead with passion or pride; it's not enough.

Your job is to find out *what* people are proud of and *why*.

These are incredible research gifts showing you where to dig next. That's when the fun really begins. It's when you find out about the real behaviors, values, and ethics of a company with a side of anecdotes and stories that give you goose bumps. It's when you see a room full of people cry because they're reliving the time when a teammate nearly died, and everyone rallied around to support them. Then you ask why again. This produces pure gold, the stuff you can't poll or survey or read about. When you get a room full of people inflow, the language they use, the descriptives, the feelings, and even the body language tell you more than an answer to one question can provide.

"There is still much work to do in the Employer Brand space with many brands using the same values and principles and not really differentiating their offer. We see overuse of the words integrity, customer-centric, collaborative, agile, to name a few. Although true, they are really what we call 'hygiene factors'—things that every organization needs to be able to exist and make a profit. Differentiated brands go deeper and get under the skin of what is unique about their culture and their people."

—JULIE RANDALL, PH.CREATIVE

A little more about perception, reality, noise, and pure gold.

Quite often, we find "perception versus reality" examples in every organization, where groups of people, or entire divisions or even geographies, have a strong perception about something that's not necessarily true. It's usually based on their personal experience or due to misaligned communications, variations of process, divisional cultures, or a lag of leadership communications and poor implementation of new initiatives. The root cause can be anything, but we find perception versus reality in every business we work with.

Being able to report on perception versus reality provides a significant amount of business intelligence outside of the remit of an employer brand. We won't get sucked into that. However, validating the results you find along the way is essential; otherwise, you risk building an employer brand and crafting an EVP on a foundation that's simply not true.

Take leaders, for example. Leaders tend to be a bit removed from the reality of the work experience because of their seniority in the organization. Therefore, leaders often perceive a current reality to be more of an aspirational version of the truth since their day to day involves taking the company forward.

Managers sometimes perceive a current reality to be more stressful than their team.

Employees often perceive a current reality of their specific work environment to be reflective of everywhere else in the company.

This means the truth isn't always what everyone expects to see as an outcome. And some will doubt it's achievable at all.

Quite often, large global organizations tell us they don't believe a universal experience exists in their organization. This can be due to their global scale, the addition of companies through acquisition, or the differences between new hires and those who have been there for decades. Time and time again, we've heard the experience of working in corporate headquarters is totally different than working in their retail stores or working as a factory worker in Haneda, Japan, for example.

"A company's EVP is as unique as a fingerprint. Identifying and showcasing what makes up your organization's DNA will assist in attracting and engaging people to consider your company as a place they could belong."

—DINA MEDEIROS, DIRECTOR OF GLOBAL
TALENT, BLIZZARD ENTERTAINMENT

With all of that said, there is a truth to be found. Design and execute the right mix of qualitative and quantitative research, and you will leave your stakeholders with the utmost confidence that what you've uncovered is the universal experience of working at your organization regardless of geography, job category, tenure, or company size.

Learning how to listen, observe, engage, and unearth key insights allows you to distill the common experiences, universal beliefs, shared values, and behaviors that can be caught, distilled, polished, crafted, verbalized, and organized into a fair reflection of who you are and why it's worth caring about.

Catching this truth isn't easy, but nothing worthwhile is. At the outset, it's like trying to catch butterflies with a broken net, but this book is designed to show exactly how to do it.

World-class employer brand development lives and dies by your ability to catch the truth at the research stage until you're confident you've seen it, heard it, and felt it.

WHY IT'S TOUGH TO CATCH "TRUTH"

If you're struggling with why it's not easy to catch truth, consider these questions:

1. Does everyone in the organization experience the same company experience?
2. Does everyone in the organization come to work for the same reasons?
3. Does everyone in the organization appreciate and prioritize the same strengths, benefits, and opportunities the organization has to offer?
4. Does every different office location feel the same as the next?
5. Are all of your hiring, engagement, and attraction challenges the same every year?

If we can agree that the answers to some, many, or all the questions above are no, then suddenly, unearthing the truth doesn't seem as easy as it did moments ago.

SUMMARY

When you're done with your research, your goal is to have an employer brand that most people own, that the organization accepts as a fair reflection of the current work experience, with a twist of an aspirational vision (operating on the law of "you can't please all the people all the time").

This means that listening, engaging, and experiencing the organization through the eyes of all your people is essential before you can begin to distill and then articulate the true experience.

In the next chapter, we'll break down the research methodology further to look at how we recommend you capture insights from employees, leaders, and the market.

RESEARCH STEPS

_____

"Never forget what you are, the rest of the world will not. Wear it like armor and it can never be used to hurt you."

—TYRION LANNISTER, *Game of Thrones*

A solid foundation of research is the key to crafting an authentic employer brand and EVP. Yet, it's not just about the current reality of the employee experience. You also need to learn about the organization's overall business strategy to determine the reality of today, the aspirations for the future, and the known challenges the organization must overcome to succeed.

Therefore, this is how we recommend organizing your research efforts:

- The business strategy
- Leadership view of the company (aspirations)
- Employee view of the company (current reality)
- Market view

We will spend time in this chapter covering each of these

areas, diving deeper into how to approach each area of your research to ensure you get the maximum value out of the engagement. But first, let's talk about why a robust methodology is so important.

ESTABLISH A BRANDING COMMITTEE

One of the first things you need to do is establish a branding committee to review and direct the work internally from strategy through to developing the final creative assets. Aim to elect five to eight executives to this committee. Members of this committee should be respected members of the company representing different service areas, offices, and points of view.

The wish list looks something like this:

- Diversity and inclusion
- Talent attraction
- Culture/purpose
- Internal communications
- Brand management
- Marketing/PR/Corporate affairs
- HR

SELECT AN AGENCY

We highly recommend using an outside partner to conduct

your research. I (Charlotte) have gone about it both ways. And I have seen, time and time again, the credibility of the project skyrockets when I have a professional partner leading this part of the work. It's frustrating, but the less-than-ideal parts of your culture that bubble up are received and accepted more when a professional branding agency delivers the news.

Early in my career, it was easy for a senior stakeholder to talk me out of what I found and change the direction of a project. Some key insights got watered down, and other pillars became so consensus-driven that it ended up being ineffective.

If you have a strong creative team internally, tap them to put flesh on the bones of your strategy. If you don't, look for an agency that when you see their work, it makes you *feel* something. People feel ten times faster than they think. If an agency plays it safe and all their work is full of stock photography, keep looking.

EMPLOYER BRAND KICKOFF WORKSHOP

Start by facilitating a two- to three-hour workshop with the core project team. The goal is to bring together those who are responsible for talent attraction, as well as those who are instrumental in shaping and influencing culture, internal communications, and recruitment strategies, to better understand current experience and areas that are being enhanced.

Be strategic with your invites; this group should be able to help socialize your work within their teams and will be key advocates when it comes time to activate.

I (Charlotte) like to get my CEO and then a click down from the C-suite in the room. I strive to have representation from all key hiring areas and divisions as the needs and challenges can vary drastically inside companies. I try to get people who have enough seniority to be respected but who are new enough to have fresh ideas and want to take the company forward. Sometimes I have found leaders with long tenure are less open to changing the way we work, so I ensure that I have a diversity of thought in the room.

Once you identify your core team, it's time to invite them to the meeting. Here's a sample invite:

> We have forged a strategy to raise our reputation externally as being considered a great place to work. As such, a clearly understood employee value proposition must be identified, validated, articulated, and ultimately activated. The labor markets in which we operate can be very competitive. Strong employer brands, like strong customer brands, stand out in the marketplace. They make it very clear why talented people should join, stay, and commit to their organizations.

We are asking you to participate in a two-hour kickoff meeting with our employer brand leader, Charlotte Marshall, as well as our agency partner, Ph.Creative, to discuss how to position our organization in the employment marketplace.

Specific discussion will center on gaining an understanding of the employment experience and challenges, and the challenges in your given market/business unit.

The complete Integrated Marketing Communication plan is attached with more background.

Thank you for your support.

An agenda typically includes:

- Review scope of work
- Verify target market hierarchy—whom you will conduct primary research with
- Logistical considerations
- Identify project teams, roles, and responsibilities
- Define secondary stakeholders to engage in project/ roles and key milestones relevant to those groups
- Clarify the approval process
- Assess materials and research available
- Information review

Next, you want to build on your existing employee-related

data, leverage the foundational elements of your company's business and corporate brand, and understand the baseline reality of how you currently communicate to employees and candidates. The following is a list of items that you'll want to gather and review with your agency:

- Corporate brand platform
- Mission, vision, business strategy, recruitment, and retention strategy
- Recent engagement surveys, employee satisfaction surveys, exit interviews, or early impression surveys
- Current recruitment advertising to target audiences
- Internal communications/newsletters
- Employee programs (learning and development, onboarding, professional development, etc.)
- Current metrics utilized and corresponding reports

LEADERSHIP INTERVIEWS

"A point of view can be a dangerous luxury when substituted for insight and understanding."

—MARSHALL MCLUHAN

Gathering the perspective of your leadership team is critical. It's your only opportunity to align your employer brand with the business strategy, so don't skip it. We typically conduct eight to ten interviews with key leaders to gain insight into the employment experience today and aspirations for the future. We recommend conducting these interviews with HR leadership and leaders/influencers who have a strategic view of business objectives, talent management, and workforce planning—division/business leads to those in the C-suite.

Each interview will last thirty to forty-five minutes and will be conducted over the phone. An interview guide will be developed by your agency partner and approved by your team in advance.

SAMPLE INTERVIEW GUIDE

Objective

Present and discuss how to position company X in the employment marketplace. Specific discussion will center on gaining an understanding of the employment experience and challenges in the given market/business unit.

Questions:

1. What resonates the most when you think about the overall goals and objectives of company X?
2. How do employees in your area fulfill our company mission?
3. How would you sell company X to a top candidate looking to join your team?

4. Describe the key reasons why employees would choose to stay at company X.

5. Describe the work environment that company X provides for its employees.

6. What is it about the "experience" of working at company X that makes it unique compared to other organizations in your industry?

7. What attributes do employees need to have to be successful at company X?

8. How would you want employees to respond to these questions:
   a. What do you get out of working for company X?
   b. How do you feel about working at company X?

9. What can company X do to ensure its recruitment process will be appealing to top talent?

10. If it was your job to convince someone not to take a job on your team and you couldn't lie, what would you say?

11. Is there anything else you would like to add that has not already been covered?

Things to keep in mind when interviewing leaders:

Leaders give you their perspective, from the top of the organization, which is typically the most forward-facing view of the employee experience, the culture, and values.

It's not uncommon for this leadership view to be aspirational. It's important to get a feel for what the aspiration of the leaders is. However, you must distinguish between aspiration and reality, which means you must dig elsewhere and discuss any disparity you find later.

To distinguish between aspiration and reality, validate the distilled answers with the rest of the audience you engage with as your research moves forward.

When considering the *Give and Get*, it's important to probe the leaders on what they expect, demand, and admire in their people. This significantly informs the Give. In fact, the leadership provides a key view of the Give part of the EVPs. This is because leaders are charged with steering the ship, determining the culture, and setting the values and behaviors they want in the company.

Probing for example stories are key because you learn a lot from the language they use, the examples they give, and the behaviors, values, actions, and achievements they appreciate. Of course, the anecdotes and tales they tell are sometimes some of the most memorable and compelling ways to use simple storytelling to make a point, land a message, or put ideas into the mix.

Talking to leaders is also essential to reinforce the value of your work. Establishing a strong, undeniable correlation between the priorities on their desks and the value your work can bring is not to be underestimated. Here's how. Collect a single insight from each leader and make sure it shows up in your work at the end. Not only is this an excellent quality assurance test to see if your work is fit for purpose, but it's also the fastest way to get sign-off, green lights, and support when it comes to activation rollout.

From every interview, your goal is to recruit another staunch advocate for your project.

EMPLOYEE SURVEY

As employer brand leaders, our goal is to leave our stake-holders with the confidence that what we land on is the universal experience. Data is your best friend when trying to identify the universal experience of working inside a company, especially in large, global organizations. We can't tell you how many times we've been told a universal experience doesn't exist. The only way to prove the commonalities is with data from a survey.

The online survey consists of twenty to thirty questions (with up to five questions being open-ended) and typically is open for a two-week period.

Topics addressed include the importance of employment experience attributes, employer delivery of employment experience attributes, competitor identification, preferred message content, and preferred message channels. Respondents are categorized by business unit/division/geography, job category, tenure, total work experience, gender, and level of engagement. Your agency partner will design, host, and report on the findings of the online survey.

Your goal is to have enough responses to your survey to be a representative sample of your total population. You can Google "sample size calculator" and use that information to determine how many people you need to interview to get results that reflect the target population. You can also find the level of precision you have in an existing sample.

Two survey questions that drive EVP differentiation:

1. What matters most to you in your career?
2. In what areas does our company deliver well?

To answer these questions, provide the following multiple-choice list of answers and ask people to choose the top five answers. Look for answers where 70 percent or more of respondents agree. This is the start of attributes that you can say matter to your entire workforce. Then look to see how well they measure your company delivering against those needs.

PURPOSE	IMPACT	BELONGING
Benefits	Challenging work	Company/product brand
Ability to move around the company	Company is global	Diversity
	Feeling a sense of achievement	Feeling included
Clear direction of the company	Learning opportunities	Ethics
Compensation	Manager quality	Flexibility of work environment
Importance of work	Training	Fun
Innovation	Advancement opportunities	Passion
Quality of product	Support for the community	Respect
Customer focus	Coworker quality	Safety
Shared mission	Open communication	Integrity of coworkers
Leadership	Empowerment of employees	Location
	Work-life balance	Stability of the company
		Teamwork

Anywhere you have an overlap between what matters most to your workforce and your company scored "good" or "exceptional" becomes a contender for your part of your *Give and Get*.

What's important to note here is the overlap you have are *not* the final answers you're looking for. The full answers you're looking for are the reasons *why* and *how* those common themes are true.

You'll notice we've categorized the multiple-choice answers into the three top human drivers: purpose, impact, and belonging. It's always interesting to see what categories most answers fall within. Sometimes it's evenly spread, but other times it overindexes on one category, which is an interesting indicator toward the type of culture you have. If there's a clear majority preference, you should keep that in mind when positioning your employer brand and EVPs.

EMPLOYEE FOCUS GROUPS

"The greatest obstacle to discovery is not ignorance—it is the illusion of knowledge."

—DANIEL J. BOORSTIN

It's important to balance out the quantitative data and the leadership view with the voice of the employee via focus groups. You can keep these universal in nature or segment your focus groups to focus on the personas you want to develop. The goal is to capture the direction, priorities, known challenges, intentions, and aspirations of the organization.

The number of sessions will range, but a general guide is to conduct six, professionally moderated two-hour sessions at company locations with eight to ten current employees per session. During the focus groups, you will discuss topics that will help you gain an understanding of the employment experience, why employees chose company X, why they choose to stay, and what their key motivators are. Your agency partner will develop a discussion guide for your approval, moderate the focus groups, and deliver a findings report.

The employee view is the most grounded feedback you will get, but it tends to be set by the tenure of the employees you're speaking to. It's a good idea to speak to different groups of employees based on tenure and segment the quantitative research results by tenure, too.

This is particularly valuable because it gives you a good indication of perceptions and trends of change across the organization, which can be extremely valuable when analyzing the results and distilling the data into key insights.

With the leadership view, the main challenge is distinguishing between the aspirational future and the reality of today. Whereas with the employee view, the main challenge is distinguishing between perception (quite often perception based on times gone by) versus reality. Sometimes it's "perception versus reality" due to opinions or biases formed on historic, outdated experiences.

We always uncover communication challenges as well, key information not reaching the general populous of the employees fast enough, or new initiatives that have yet to be launched. For whatever the reason, we always find there's an element of "perception versus reality," and so it's essential to validate the results of the employee view with leadership to determine what's valuable insight and what's noise getting in the way of building something valuable and truly authentic.

The employee view is where you determine most insights surrounding the realities of the Give and the Get. If the Give is coming out differently to that offered up by the leaders, and it's more than just semantics; there could be a need for change management, which can be baked into your employer brand by creating and acknowledging an aspirational EVP specifically to inspire change.

When probing to discover the employee Give, the most important insight you can hope to glean is a collective sense of what sacrifices and commitments must be made and why they make them. Getting to the bottom of this, amid an array of different employee experiences, is the ultimate holy grail of your work.

Unsurprisingly, the employees often provide the most insightful view of the Get part of the EVPs, not because they know the most in terms of what's on offer at the organization, but because they can provide the most accurate insight surrounding what they value the most.

Quite often, you discover amid a plethora of expensive benefits, facilities, rewards, schemes, and initiatives, it's the simple things people value most.

For both the Give and the Get, it always comes down to how people feel. Capturing how people feel because of all your research can mean the difference between merely collecting data and the ability to extract valuable new insight from your work.

FINDING STORY GOLD

The workshops and focus groups are a story gold mine. Be ready to capture notes, names, and examples because the examples that come up in these sessions reveal the stories that you need to tell externally to activate your EVP.

Here are a few of the questions we ask to find stories in focus groups:

- What are the most moving stories you've heard about working here?
- Describe your best day at work? How does it feel?
- What happened/happens on your worst?
- When you need to remotivate yourself after a bad day at work, what do you remind yourself of?
- Why do you do what you do?
- If it was your job to convince someone not to work here (and you couldn't lie), what would you say?
- How do you describe your job to your kids (or nieces/ nephews)?
- When did you know you wanted to work here?
- When did you know you made the right decision to join this company?

- Tell me about the work environment and culture. What is it like to work here?
- In one word, describe the people you work with. Why did you choose that word?
- Why do you stay here?
- What makes you feel like you belong here?
- What impact do you have on this company?
- What has been your proudest career moment here?
- Can you describe your most memorable shared moment at this company?

THE MARKET VIEWS

"Facts do not cease to exist because they are ignored."

—ALDOUS HUXLEY

Differentiating your employer brand among your talent competitors is the number one reason to compare yourself against what your talent competitors are saying.

If you think about it, of course you'll be differentiated— you're different. No two corporate cultures on earth are the same. But then again, how many employer brand headlines have you read and thought, "We could say that about our company" or "Big deal. So what?"

Being accurate and truthful is important, but accuracy will

get you only so far. Accuracy on its own can be boring and uninspiring.

Like any sort of branding and storytelling, you can either be interesting, engaging, and compelling or not. In this case, we want an employer brand that differentiates for several priority reasons; attention, affinity, and authenticity are all arguably far more important than worrying about being the most generally attractive.

Ask yourself a series of questions that will help you set parameters and guardrails throughout the employer brand development process.

- What do they all claim?
- What words do they all tend to use?
- What is strong about the competition that can't be ignored?
- Does it speak to purpose, impact, or belonging?
- Does it promote a point of view?

BENCHMARKING YOUR CURRENT PERFORMANCE

The second reason for including a robust market view in your research is to ensure you know what you're up against in the marketplace. The level of sophistication, resource, engagement, and effectiveness your talent competitors are achieving is an important factor for a variety of reasons.

- What can we see that is clearly working to get the attention of the talent we'd like to have?
- How much of our resources is it going to take to get the attention of the talent we want to reach?
- What other considerations do we need to have to win our unfair share of the best talent in the world?
- What other considerations do we need to have to keep our valued talent?

EASILY ACCESSIBLE THINGS TO REVIEW

- Glassdoor ratings and reviews summary
- Social media engagement levels reach and brand sentiment
- Sophistication of their careers website (user interface design/user experience design, messaging, positioning, voice of the employee, clarity)
- Level of engagement and consistency of their job adverts/descriptions
- Compelling nature of their LinkedIn profiles

"When it comes to your employer branding—if you don't stand out, you're not worth thinking about. We see our employer brand as a chance to let our current and prospective employees know that they have the chance to be a part of something different from us.

"Start with identifying the white space in your industry; look

at your peers and what they say about themselves and use that as a jumping-off point to create something you haven't seen before. Obviously, it's got to be true, so the real challenge is to tell the truth as creatively as you can from a unique perspective that no one else could replicate or live up to. Be you, be unique, and be brave enough to be purple."

—GRAEME JOHNSON, DIRECTOR OF RESOURCING
AND EMPLOYER BRAND STRATEGY, GVC PLC

A LESSON LEARNED FROM RESEARCHING THE MARKET VIEW

The absence of data is often more telling than the data available to you. The answers you're looking for might not be what is there but rather what is missing.

Blizzard Entertainment is one of the biggest and most respected games development companies in the world; they are adored and admired. The community is insanely engaged and passionate about this company and the games they produce.

To work at Blizzard and have a hand in creating the games is an incredible honor, and it's considered a much sought-after privilege.

When speaking to the art department, Ph.Creative learned that they had difficulty recruiting junior workers. For some reason, they did not get many applications that were near the standard they knew to exist in the marketplace. This was a small, yet growing, concern, because they needed fresh young talent to bring through the ranks and maintain their high levels of quality and creativity. Without that, they would start to decline.

When Ph.Creative spoke to the junior art workers who had recently joined, they were puzzled, too. They confirmed the reputation of Blizzard Entertainment and reaffirmed the external perception, given they had only recently joined the organization. At this point, we could have concluded that there is simply more competition for the young talent, and we would have to try harder to demonstrate the benefits and opportunities of choosing Blizzard over a competitor.

But this would have been a big mistake.

Up until this point, we had neglected to conduct our "market view" research, and so of course, these junior workers were the same as the returning planes in the introduction to this book. We had to speak to the junior artists who didn't apply to Blizzard in the first place. And so we did.

It turns out that Blizzard Entertainment has such an incredible reputation in the marketplace that some people were waiting up to ten years too long to apply for a position at Blizzard for fear of not being good enough.

Armed with this new information, Ph.Creative asked different questions of the artists to confirm a level of imposter syndrome in every artist, even the ones who have been there for years. "I worry I'll be told I'm not good enough all the time. I look around at my amazing peers and fear I'll be found out every day," said one artist we talked to (who was amazing, by the way).

There was an abundance of new insights to be drawn from this new aspect of external research. The obvious starting point was that the stories of the Blizzard employees should narrate how the artists felt when they started out and how they still feel now—they all have imposter syndrome. With this insight, we can be sure to empathize with potential candidates as well as demonstrate the incredible learning journey they go on to get better and better over time—you don't need to be the finished article to apply.

Further investigation and validation then led to the conclusion that the EVP we created would have to be extremely open, inclusive, human, and approachable. Blizzard was a victim of its own success, and the right EVP could be designed to overcome it.

The people are all generally humble and first and foremost servants to the team and the shared cause of creating great games. Because of this, the employer brand essence heavily leaned into a palpable shared passion and a deeply cherished sense of belonging.

HOW TO PRESENT YOUR RESEARCH ROADMAP INTERNALLY

Download this IMC plan: ph-creative.com/IMCplan.

It's a great document to personalize and use during your immersion meetings with key stakeholders. It articulates what you are doing and the tactics and timing it will take to get to the finish line.

SUMMARY

"Nothing is more terrible than activity without insight," according to Thomas Carlyle. We agree. The distinction between data and insights is the most important takeaway from this chapter.

Creating insights on which to build your employer brand isn't as easy as reading data and seeing how it stacks up. There's a science to research, but there's an art to creating new insight. We believe valuable insights are created when you reach a new or different conclusion based on a deep understanding of the information available to you *and* the gaps in between the data, too.

If you can read multiple data points, study the gaps, and come up with your own equation that results in a new "therefore," you just might be onto something.

When you set out to plan your research methodology, ensure you capture the following:

- The business strategy
- Leadership view of the company (aspirations)
- Employee view of the company (current reality)
- Market view

Next, we turn our focus to personas—a great way to understand your talent audience on a deeper level to create more meaningful experiences. After all, each segment of your audience has different priorities, preferences, and perspectives. If you know what they are, you can match your communications to them with much greater effect.

PERSONA DEVELOPMENT AND THE *GIVE AND GET* FOR CRITICAL TALENT

———

"Education is an ornament in prosperity and a refuge in adversity."

—ARISTOTLE

PERSONA DEVELOPMENT AND AUDIENCE SEGMENTATION

A persona is an archetypal representation of each audience segment. The insights we can gather provide you with the opportunity to create an infinitely more meaningful brand experience for your internal and external talent audience because when you are done, you can hit all the right notes—the different priorities of each audience segment—to create more affinity with your audience.

The theory is, by recognizing that your audience is made up of different types of people wanting different things, we create tailored experiences to enable personalization every step of the way. The alternative is one generic brand experience bearing the weight of responsibility to engage with everyone.

Understanding our talent audience on a deeper level allows us to create meaningful experiences. Each segment of our audience has different priorities, preferences, and perspectives. If we know what they are, we can match our communications to them with much greater effect.

For example, when talking to software engineers, they might be attracted to your organization primarily because of the complex challenges they will work on, the latest technology available to them, and having access to smart people. Working long hours doesn't faze them, but bureaucracy and slow decision making is something that frustrates them.

A sales executive at the same organization might be more motivated by the impact your product has on the world, and the benefits and compensation on offer. Their biggest turnoffs are working long hours, traveling constantly, and being responsible for their own performance with very little structure to support them.

These may all be strengths, benefits, and harsh realities of your organization, but doesn't it make sense to lead with a different, more tailored proposition for each of the candidates now that we know what they care about most?

It's not that we're saying different things to different people to appear more attractive; rather, we're positioning things slightly differently, reordering information to match what your audience cares about the most.

By taking the time to understand each persona, you can discover the unique motivators, drivers, preferences, and priorities behind each one so that when it comes to communicating and engaging with them, you know what, when, where, and how to deliver a message in the most meaningful and relevant way possible.

USING PERSONA INSIGHTS TO CREATE MORE IMPACT WITH AN OVERALL GLOBAL MESSAGING

Have you ever wondered why the *Avengers* movies have been so successful? The audience appeal is incredible. From three-year-old boys and girls to grown men and women, even your nan loves the *Avengers*. Why? It's because each one of the characters has been specifically designed to appeal to a different segment of the public. It's usually easy for people to name their favorite Avenger; it's the one that's been designed to resonate with them the most.

In case you're wondering, Charlotte loves Black Widow and Hawk-Eye, and Bryan loves Iron Man and Pepper Potts (the most underappreciated semi-Avenger of them all).

When you add up all the appeals that each character creates with their segment of the audience, it results in one of the biggest, most beloved movie franchises on earth.

How did Hollywood do it? They took the time to get to know every segment of the general audience, and they injected specific insights into each character so that every person watching could identify with at least one of the heroes on the screen in front of them.

MARKETING VERSUS TALENT ATTRACTION AND ENGAGEMENT

If you have ever had the pleasure of seeing someone from Fairygodboss speak at an event, they talk about the value of presenting your organization in a more inclusive light to attract top female talent.

To make their point on stage, they sometimes talk about Dove antiperspirant and the fact that they package their antiperspirant product using two different variations: a black one for men and a white one for women. The messaging and presentation of the product is subtly different on each label, despite the product being the same.

Why does Dove do this? It's because they understand the power of creating a brand experience that is tailored to each segment of their audience. They understand that for this one product to be inclusively appealing to the entire adult consumer audience, they need to present it in two different ways.

Dove is not selling different products to each audience segment, but they are telling a slightly different story to each one, based on what they know to be most appealing to each audience segment.

By taking the time to both understand and empathize more with each side of the audience, Dove creates more market appeal and sells more units as a result. It's both smart and considerate of the audience.

Since the early 2010s when the phrase "Recruiters need to think more like marketers" was being repeated on what seemed like every conference stage on earth, the recruitment sector, influenced by the rise of inbound marketing, slowly started to adopt persona development on a more widespread scale.

With every employer brand we develop, we identify anything from four to twenty-four different personas (and beyond) so we can create a more intimate, empathetic, and specific understanding of each type of person in your organization, just like our marketing friends.

However, there are also big differences with how we use

those audience insights when it comes to marketing to a consumer audience versus engaging with a talent audience.

When you think about it, there is an obvious difference between the intentions of your sales team and your TA team.

The objective of marketing is to increase the size of the audience as much as possible and to create a sale from every prospective customer. Every time a member of their audience wants to buy something, without question they make the sale.

With talent attraction, it's virtually the complete opposite. A large proportion of the talent audience wants to "buy" what you have to offer; however, they will likely be rejected. We don't sell to everyone. We don't give a job to everyone who applies, and so to simply increase the volume of the audience is in complete contrast to our marketing friends.

Can you imagine your sales and marketing department rejecting 99 percent of the customers who wanted to buy from them? Neither can we.

Have you ever met a head of talent attraction who wants more applications? We have not. But every head of talent would welcome more of the right applications, right? If we could create a reality whereby the overall applications reduced but the qualified applications remained the same or even increased, what would be the ideal scenario for talent attraction?

REPEL THE MANY, ATTRACT THE FEW

Our job is to use the persona insights to assist the audience in making a more informed decision whether to apply or not. The best-case scenario is that people who are not qualified and people who would not thrive in the culture of your organization do not apply. We owe it to the organization to reduce the noise amid the cost and time associated with a high application volume, and we owe it to the candidate to make a sound career progression decision.

Imagine knowing the types of people who thrive in your organization so well that you can train your recruiters and hiring managers to spot them within seconds. Imagine being able to search them out with a high degree of accuracy and market to them specifically in such a way that your message deeply resonates and compels them to either apply or to remain motivated to work for you.

The best way to achieve this is to be able to articulate your EVP in a meaningful way with a clear *Give and Get*.

So let's get started with how to create an effective persona to use within your employer brand.

HOW DO YOU CHOOSE WHICH AUDIENCE SEGMENTS TO DEVELOP INTO A PERSONA?

When you have a large organization, with lots of employees doing a wide variety of roles, it can be difficult to decide whom to focus on as part of your initial research.

Persona development can and should be something you're constantly doing to get to know your talent audience better. On an annual basis, you should be prepared to test your existing insights to ensure they're still valid, to supplement them with new insights, and to ensure you're staying relevant.

Behaviors, habits, language, priorities, as well as your own business strategy can change frequently, and so relying on inaccurate specifics can be as much a risk as not having research to base your work on at all.

Typically, you will have a variety of known priority challenges within your organization, so that's the best place to start. Try answering the questions below to help you identify the most pressing and priority personas to develop first:

1. **What new talent are you hiring for or will be hiring for soon that you haven't hired in the past?** As your organization changes, it's not uncommon to have to hire new positions that you are not familiar with at all. For that to be a successful endeavor, it would be

highly recommended to add these groups of roles to the priority list.

2. **What people do you hire for who tend to have a much higher attrition rate than general?** This would suggest there's a challenge with expectations, environmental conditions, or something that's not being suitably satisfied for them to stay longer.

3. **What groups of talent consistently take an above-average time or cost to hire?** This would indicate that you could benefit from a greater level of insight to find and attract suitable people in a more effective and efficient manner. This could be simply discovering where they typically hang out online, or even finding insights that could help drive referral campaigns internally, and so forth.

4. **What groups of people consistently score low on employee engagement surveys?** Persona mapping these groups of people can be incredibly revealing. Not only can it provide answers to how you could optimize the working environment better for them, but it can also help you learn more about character traits, personality types, or experience that could make all the difference in how you engage and reward these people or how you choose to bring in and screen out during their candidate experience.

5. **What roles are you always hiring for?** Sometimes the volume hires are overlooked because the numbers are consistent and there is not an obvious problem or chal-

lenge with how it's going. However, it could be that it's this group of people that is responsible for defining your culture the most and even helping you find more talent around them. If you take the time to develop these personas, it could have a huge impact on your attraction and retention performance, year on year.

6. **What roles are becoming increasingly more difficult to fill or retain?** Sometimes there are roles in your organization that are becoming more and more difficult to fill due to a rise in competition, a change in industry, politics, or the economy. Whatever the reason, it's beneficial to get ahead of the challenge. The more you know about this audience segment, the better, for obvious reasons.

7. **Is there any group of people you consistently lose to a specific competitor?** If the answer to this question is yes and your organization happens to value them, it's a priority contender for persona development. In many organizations we've worked with, *talent flow* between specific talent competitors becomes a vital employer brand metric once we're done, specifically to see if we can create change in this area.

If you're unsure of the answers to these questions, speak to your recruiters, hiring managers, division leaders, and managers—they will tell you where they're having difficulties. This approach also tends to raise awareness of your employer brand work and increase peer buy-in and interest to your work, too.

GEOGRAPHIC, SENIORITY, AND TENURE DIFFERENCES

When deciding on your primary list of personas, dig into as much detail as possible to discover who the priority personas are.

If there's a company-wide requirement for software developers in multiple locations, that's one thing. If you require software developers in Israel only, that's a completely different task at hand. Similarly, you should be specific about seniority and any known prerequisites around experience for the same reason. A graduate software engineer in Boston is a different prospect from a senior software engineer with years of industry experience.

The final consideration is whether it's more of the same talent you have or a completely new type of talent you want. This is essential to understand because your approach to developing the persona is different if it's a new talent you don't yet already have.

HOW PERSONAS HAVE EVOLVED IN RECENT YEARS TO SOLVE FOR DIVERSITY AND INCLUSION

At the inception of persona development, there was a basic premise that the more specific you could be about bringing your persona to life, the more you got to know your audience segment, the better you could market to them. This premise still holds water today; however, the execution of the theory has changed radically over the years.

At Ph.Creative, we have evolved our thinking way beyond the conventional makeup, and since around 2015, we have been experimenting and refining an approach away from the typical persona profile, which used to look something like this:

"Marketing Molly"

Thirty-two years old, has two children, lives with her husband just outside of the city, drives a Volkswagen, and loves yoga, jogging, and socializing with friends.

So why has our approach changed recently? We found that although our personas were delivering insights to enable us to focus on a much more targeted segment of a talent audience when it came to diversity, we were striking out. These traditional personas are littered with a bias that, while being effective, reduced the talent pool so extensively that organizations naturally miss out on the positive impact of the diverse candidate.

We don't pay attention to demographics or a tangible, visual makeup of an ideal candidate. Instead, we focus on building a targeted ideal of mindset, capability, ethos, behaviors, and values, which opens a completely new realm of possibility for inclusion and diversity as well as more transactional and functional benefits to making the hiring process more efficient and effective.

The Building Blocks of a Modern Persona Profile
- A persona narrative/description
- Primary/unique identifiers (can be an exec summary of other points below)
- Key motivators and drivers
- Personality and character
- Behaviors and values
- Goals (personal and professional)
- Online and offline habits and routines
- Preferences and interests/frustrations and pain points
- Core skills and abilities
- Language, buzzwords, and keywords
- Quotes, stories, and proof points

How much detail? What level of role specificity do we go to?

The simple answer to these questions is, it's up to you. The more specific you are, the more tailored you can be and so the better the results you'll get.

With high-priority talent segments, we recommend being as specific as the job category. There are many different types of software engineers, so creating a persona for everyone is impractical for most organizations. This is a good example of how you might group all software engineers together to begin with. You can always go deeper if required.

That said, you do need to record the different nuances of seniority, tenure, and location. Try using a simple matrix such as the one below to capture the key differences for each of these to supplement an overall "software engineer" persona.

PERSONA NUANCE MATRIX

Software Engineer	Geography	Tenure
Emerging talent	Israel	Less than 3 years
		3+ years
	USA	Less than 3 years
		3+ years
Experienced talent	Israel	Less than 3 years
		3+ years
	USA	Less than 3 years
		3+ years
Senior exec talent	Israel	Less than 3 years
		3+ years
	USA	Less than 3 years
		3+ years

Question Checklist

When it comes to designing the questions to ask during your persona research, we can give you a good steer; however, we do not advocate simply using a list of stock questions you read in any book. Why? Because your organization is different from all others, and the purpose of the research at this point is to uncover the common ground between your environment and the makeup of a person who can and will thrive within. Therefore, there should always be an element of tailoring and refinement based on the company-wide research you have already carried out and the insights you have gleaned as a result.

That said, given that we know the three primary areas of resolve candidates and employees are looking to satisfy are purpose, impact, and belonging, we can use the following table to ensure we've covered all the questions required to build a persona based on the unique culture of your organization and the specific insights you have already uncovered.

BELONGING

Ethics, social conscience	Inclusion and diversity
Culture and values	Team and people
Working environment	Brand perception and reputation

IMPACT

Company benefits and reward	Technology and resources
Compensation	Career mobility
Management and structure	

PURPOSE

Mission and vision	Learning and development
Stability and consistency	Mentorship
	Innovation

THE BIG QUESTIONS

For every persona you develop, there are fundamental questions we would urge you to consider to be able to satisfy the basic needs and desires of your ideal talent audience.

Seeking insights about your persona as a human:

- What are you passionate about, and what's important to you in life?
- Why were you put on the earth?
- How do people typically describe your nature?
- Where and what makes you feel at home the most?
- What were the last three books you read?
- In a typical hour of online surfing, where do you go (and why)?

- In a typical hour of free time without Wi-Fi, what do you do?
- What are your personal priorities and preferences in life?

Seeking insights about your persona in working life:

- What motivates you to come to work the most?
- What drives you toward achieving the most?
- What do you love doing more than anything else?
- What are you best at?
- What skills and experience do you rely on the most in your role?
- What are your professional priorities and preferences at work?
- How do you like to work with others?

Seeking insights about your persona's perspective on your organization:

- What interpersonal skills, personality traits, and characteristics are required to thrive here?
- What benefits and opportunities do you appreciate the most at your company?
- What tough challenges do you relish and derive satisfaction from?
- What do you love about your role the most?
- What's the best-kept secret of your organization?

- What makes you happy here the most often?
- What do you need in terms of environment, resources, and structure to be set up for success?
- How do you feel on a typical best and worst day?

THE PERSONA RESEARCH MIX

We recommend including the following activities in your research mix:

- Internal persona survey
- A workshop
- One-on-one interview
- Focus groups
- External market research

INTERNAL PERSONA SURVEY

The survey is your chance to capture the voice of your persona population far and wide, which is essential to discover what is consistent across the business and what changes based on geography or specific conditions of teams, divisions, projects, and/or office locations. Ideally, a 10 percent uptake is the minimum response rate from your persona survey audience when you send it to five hundred or more. If you have only a small number of any persona, try to increase that percentage as much as possible. For example, if you have only fifty people making up a persona, try to get more than half of them to complete the survey and make sure there are more than five people from each different office or location.

We recommend doing the survey first. Once you distill the results, you have the basis on which to refine and build your remaining research activities and efforts. Use the survey as an informed signpost for where and what to ask people next. Knowing where to dig in more can be the difference in uncovering the important insights that matter the most or not.

Most of the questions should be quantitative questions, which means your audience is simply choosing from pre-determined choices, either/or answers, or scales from 1 to 10 or "strongly agree to strongly disagree," or even just "Yes" or "No."

For example:

How easy is it to do your best work here? 1–10

For the open-ended questions, be aware that you're creating a big task of distillation. Being concise, specific, and focused is essential to make that distillation time worthwhile. For example, here's a three-part question we like to ask to ensure we're getting a well-rounded answer to a question, and we make it easy to distill it down to something useful, too.

In as few words as possible, describe what it feels like to work here on:

Your best day: _____

A typical day: _____

The worst day: _____

THE WORKSHOP

For the workshop, we recommend up to fifteen people in attendance, in person. Of the fifteen people, include a couple of specialist recruiters who talk to the personas all day and have a good understanding of their wants, challenges, reservations, and typical questions and concerns. It's also worth noting any ideas and suggestions they might have for making it easier for them to engage and converse with this specific audience in the future. Not only will it help the effectiveness and efficiency of the recruiters, but they will also reward you with becoming stronger brand ambassadors with tools and resources that ensure a more positive and consistent branded candidate experience, too.

If you have hiring managers and team leaders in the room, we recommend not having their direct reports in the room; otherwise, people tend to start saying what they think they're supposed to say, rather than what they really feel.

Your survey questions and answers should serve as a solid basis to guide the conversation, so you can dig into answers deeper, validating ideas and assumptions or anything unexpected that's shown up in the results you have to date.

Beyond that, pick and choose the most relevant and valuable questions from the suggestions earlier and layer in specific questions to validate the wider employer brand research to date. Look to validate common themes of the wider audience, and capture the subtle differences in language, preference, and priority so you know how to tailor and order messaging later.

The value of your workshop comes down to your ability to dig for gold when you see or hear it. Following up with *why* questions and asking for tangible examples and stories to illustrate their points will provide a whole new layer of rich storytelling, which will bring your insights to life afterward.

We typically go between having group discussions and individual contributions (using sticky notes), depending on the sensitivity of the questions and answers you're expecting. Sometimes people are more comfortable writing answers down than shouting them out.

When you are facilitating the workshop, if you can, have someone record key points, answers, and insights, leaving someone free to focus on driving meaningful conversation and keeping to the agenda and time. If you can, include your member of the team who will be following up to do some one-on-one interviews to explore the brief stories uncovered in the session. Building familiarity and rapport at this stage makes it easier to extract stories and further insights later because there is an element of trust and confidence that has already been established.

ONE-ON-ONE INTERVIEW

If the workshop was a refinement of the survey, the one-on-one interview is where you react to the insights and specifics of your workshop. This is your chance to go deep—find great story examples of the highs and lows, challenges, strengths, benefits, and the harsh realities that exist within your organization for this persona.

You do not have to interview someone who was present in the workshop, but the assumptions and findings must be relatable and easy for your interviewee to grasp if not.

We like to treat the one-on-one session as consultations, seeking advice and guidance with how to shape the work we're doing to make it more genuine and authentic and how to make it resonate with more impact, meaning, and purpose.

We often get feedback that the individual interviews feel like a therapy session, where people have gotten things off their chest and felt better for the discussion. This is a very good sign! If you can elicit this sort of response, you have probably done a very good job, and as a reward, you will have found yourself a strong employee advocate who will be willing to proactively do what they can to help you launch your employer brand when the time comes.

All your participants should be kept in the loop and shown that their contribution is appreciated and valued. If you do that, they will repay you with all the help you ask for to launch your new employer brand, which is good because it takes a village.

FOCUS GROUPS

What better way to keep people in the loop than with a focus group to determine "Did we hear you right? Is this what you said?"

Your focus groups should be used once you have had time to distill your research down into key insights and common themes that you have found to date. It's also your opportunity to clarify anything that's unclear or ambiguous in your findings.

If you have any early creative ideas, now is also the time

to float them for the first time to see what hits and what misses the mark.

The key to making the best use of your focus group time is to remain unbiased, removing emotion or any strong preferences or theories you and your team have already begun to formulate. Test, but you must resist the temptation to influence your audience, or you run the risk of getting your work completely wrong.

Try mixing your ideas among others, frame your findings using clean language, and present findings as simply as possible, paying attention to the reaction you get and the comments you receive.

EXTERNAL PERSONA RESEARCH

Just like the research we recommend for the main employer brand, understanding the external persona view is equally important and extremely valuable to validate and cross-check against the internal insights you gather.

Sometimes you will be hiring talent that creates a new persona entirely, and so external research is all you can do.

If it turns out that the reason you're not attracting the right level or volume of high-caliber talent is that you're not competitive enough or there's a brand perception issue, then that information is essential to your talent attraction efforts. It may even mean there's a fundamental change required outside of the employer brand remit altogether.

In some situations, talent is so sought after that the proposition needs to be designed based on what it takes to attract those select few. External research will tell you exactly what you have to offer to become an attractive proposition.

HOW TO APPLY THE *GIVE AND GET* TO PERSONA INSIGHTS TO TURBOCHARGE YOUR EVP

The following table breaks down top-level needs and desires you must be able to satisfy in the simplest terms that will give you the critical insights to formulate a meaningful *Give and Get*.

PERSONA

What the persona is looking for	What the persona needs to possess to thrive
Priority motivators and drivers	Primary characteristics
Priority aspects of belonging	Realities of the employee experience
	Character, personality, and perspective
Priority aspects of impact	Capabilities
Priority aspects of purpose	Values, beliefs, and behaviors

To create meaningful *Give and Get* messaging for a persona, you must have a true understanding of what they want and need so you can balance it with a true reflection of what it takes to achieve what they're searching for.

With every employer brand pillar, you should be able to add a layer of these priority details to make each pillar much more meaningful and useful when it comes to communicating with that persona.

For example, imagine the information found in the table below was a distillation of your research. See if you can complete the sentence to be found underneath the table and then write out what you think the *Give and Get* is in as few words as possible.

CLIENT ORGANIZATION: St. Andrews Hospital

EMPLOYER BRAND ESSENCE:	Every second counts	
EMPLOYER BRAND PILLAR:	Make a real difference	

NURSE PERSONA: INSIGHTS FROM RESEARCH	WHAT THE PERSONA NEEDS TO POSSESS/ KNOW TO THRIVE	WHAT THE PERSONA IS LOOKING FOR MOST
	Cope with long periods of stress	To be heard and included
	Be decisive under pressure	To be able to trust and be trusted
	Put others before yourself	To have room to use their experience to best effect
	See things through to the end	
	Be your own toughest critic	To be able to disagree safely
	Stick to strict quality assurance no matter what	To be supported and appreciated
	Accept the role doesn't pay as much as other roles	To see the results of the efforts put in
	Understand most of your efforts go unnoticed or formally acknowledged	To achieve recognized results that really matter to others
	Often deal with hostile, unpleasant people with empathy and caring	Contribute to continual improvement

EMPLOYER BRAND PILLAR EVP *GIVE AND GET*	WHAT THE PERSONA MUST *GIVE*	WHAT THE PERSONA CAN *GET*
	Resilience, empathy, service, commitment, team support, curiosity, determination, high integrity, composure	Recognition, contribution, trust, job satisfaction, reward, close bond with team

Start by creating some simple and basic *Give and Get* sentence constructs:

To _____ you must be willing to _____.

Here, you can _____ if you can ___

_____.

If you want to really _____, you must be able to _____.

Once you're comfortable with the basic premise of the primary value exchange for the pillar, try writing a more informative persona story to include more details about the environment, the people, and what's possible if someone is comfortable with the value exchange.

Here's an example of an overarching story to illustrate the pillar in the example above:

> *When you save someone's life, you don't need the words "thank you" to feel like you've made a difference; you can usually see it in their eyes or their parents' sigh of relief. A scared, helpless smile or even anger and frustration with the world is sometimes all the reminder you get that the work you do means the difference between comfort or discomfort, peace or torment, or even life and death.*

> *When you've worked more hours than an average body can take, you go home and fall asleep exhausted, yet proud and extremely well-compensated for your day—not by the salary but by the clear and obvious difference you make in people's lives. It's this that drives you forward; it's this that reminds you to check your*

work one more time and to take a deep breath and concentrate before facing the seventh unpleasant scenario of the day. We look around at our teammates and we recognize and respect the resilience and humility, because it's in us all as standard.

If you can be decisive under pressure, committed to doing the right thing, and composed enough to lead people through some of life's most emotionally charged highs and lows, you will find a dedicated and sharp team at your back, relying on you as much as you rely on them. You improve systems together, you push standards together, you save lives together, and it's all in a day's work.

To make a real difference here, you must be willing to work harder than most people can on the understanding that the demands, expectations, and consequences are higher than most places, too.

Once those tiny details are understood, you're ready to make the world a healthier, happier place for everyone around you, for today and for tomorrow.

What's your reaction to the story above? Our reaction is, we couldn't do that job in a million years. But for some people, it's all they can think about and the harsh realities make it more compelling, not less.

- Does the picture we paint prepare someone for the realities they will find?

- Does the story balance the upside to the sacrifice and commitment they will have to endure?
- Does the information allow the audience to make an educated decision as to whether they could thrive or just survive in that role?
- Can the audience imagine belonging, finding purpose, and/or making an impact?

What else do we do with our persona insights?

If you think once your employer brand is complete that your persona profiling days are over and these insights can be archived to your Google Drive folder, think again.

These persona insights can now help form the basis for any initiative that requires engaging with this audience segment. From experience mapping and designing a tailored candidate experience to developing a more effective talent attraction or referral campaign, these insights and "master messages" should feature heavily in your thinking across the board.

In fact, now that you know this persona so well, we encourage you to test and measure a variety of pilot campaigns to keep enriching your knowledge with what works and what doesn't.

It's not uncommon to design specific employer brand

launch activities that involve the engagement of these persona audiences, and the conversation and content you generate internally can be the most powerful ammunition for external talent attraction, too, especially if you've been brave enough to lean into specific examples and stories of how your employees have overcome adversity and harsh realities to attain what they appreciate most about your organization.

"Many companies have several different cultures inside their organizations and struggle to find commonality. These 'microcultures' often are comprised of similar types of people; that is where the true connection resides. When you craft an employer's story based on the microcultures of their teams, it feels transparent and honest. You are more likely to deliver a job and brand promise that is closer to the reality of the job a candidate applies for than just trying to sell the whole company for each position. This can fix retention rates and should lead to a more efficient hiring process."

—CRAIG FISHER, ALLEGIS GLOBAL SOLUTIONS

SUMMARY

Taking the time to understand the most critical talent segments you are trying to attract on a persona level allows you the ability to uncover their unique motivators, drivers, preferences, and priorities. This in turn gives you a roadmap for what key messages to dial up or down in your outreach.

- A modern persona profile
- A persona narrative/description
- Primary/unique identifiers (can be an exec summary of other points below)
- Key motivators and drivers
- Personality and character
- Behaviors and values
- Goals (personal and professional)
- Online and offline habits and routines
- Preferences and interests/frustrations and pain points
- Core skills and abilities
- Language, buzzwords, and keywords
- Quotes, stories, and proof points

Like your employer brand and EVP research, we recommend including the following activities in your persona research mix:

- Internal persona survey
- Workshop
- One-on-one interview
- Focus groups
- External market research

In the next chapter, we dive headfirst into storytelling. And there is no better time, because now that your research is complete, you'll get to start the EVP development process. And after you are done, the difference between good and world-class sits squarely on your ability to effectively wield the power of story.

BRING YOUR EVP TO LIFE THROUGH PURPOSE TOLD STORIES

"Storytelling is the most powerful way to put ideas into the world."

—ROBERT MCKEE

THE GOAL OF STORY

Have you ever watched a movie and felt your heart racing or had to wipe tears from the corner of your eyes?

Have you ever listened to your friend tell a joke and laughed out loud, or gotten goose bumps from the recounting of spooky coincidence?

Of course you have, because that's what a well-told story does to us. It affects us emotionally, and it can change our physical state—and can even become imprinted and memorable.

When we watch a good movie or read a good book, we get swept away. We vicariously feel what it's like to be those characters experiencing their life and the situations they find themselves in. For however long we're engaged, we're feeling what it's like to be them. In the safety of our homes or movie theaters, we get scared, feel the rush of adrenaline or the pain of loss—because for the briefest of moments, while we're in their world, we become the hero in the story.

A purpose told story is a little different. If there is a lesson to be found within a story, at the very moment the audience is feeling what it's like to be the hero, they're also feeling what's it like to learn the lesson, to see the world through their eyes and understand the motivation and desires they're experiencing, too.

Those lessons and messages become unforgettable. Your brain confuses the story with real experience and the emotions that go along with it.

Since the dawn of time, before we could write or record the wisdom of life experience, we have passed learning from generation to generation using the simple mechanics of story.

The story of the Trojan horse is a story I (Bryan) will never forget. I remember my primary school teacher reading the story to our class, and we listened, in silence, wide-eyed, hanging on every word. For those of you who may not be familiar with the tale, the Greeks pretended to sail away from Troy, leaving behind the big wooden horse containing an elite force of men including Odysseus. There they waited until nightfall, and the Trojans, believing the horse was left as a victory trophy, pulled the horse into their city. That night, the Greek force crept out of the horse and opened the gates for the rest of the Greek army, which had sailed back under the cover of the night. The Greeks entered and destroyed the city of Troy, ending the war.

When the story was over, I remember the teacher asking the class what we thought of the story and what we thought would happen if another wooden horse was presented outside of the city gates. "Don't let them in. Leave it outside!" we all shouted. "Why?" the teacher asked. "Because it's a trap."

Very quickly, the teacher managed to teach us a valuable life lesson. Metaphorically, a "Trojan horse" meant a trick, something not to be trusted. If it looks too good to be true, we should be wary of it.

The teacher could have saved some time and simply gathered us together and said, "If something looks too good to be true, be wary of it." But if she had, I doubt any of us would have learned that lesson in a profound way. Using such a gripping story meant it stayed with me forever, and I bet it's the same for all my school friends.

"At the center of all stories are people. Advertisers and marketers can create narratives around products, but we can only tell stories about people. At the heart of employer branding, there are human beings, human beings united by a set of universal aspirations and needs: to feel valued, to live a meaningful life, to forge human relationships in which respect and support is reciprocal, to be fulfilled—to be happy. All of these needs exist both outside and inside of the workplace, and often they are satisfied most significantly through the work we do."

—NICK MOSS

WHY STORY IS AN ESSENTIAL INGREDIENT TO YOUR EMPLOYER BRAND AND EVP

When you create the written architecture of your employer brand, it must be accurate. But more than that, it must effectively move people. Your words must reflect on what it *feels* like to be part of your organization.

Your employer brand must resonate with your internal audience in such a way that they proudly agree with what it's like to belong and contribute to your organization's purpose.

A good employer brand can remind people *why* they do what they do. A world-class employer brand gives you the power to recruit willing advocates, ambassadors, and brand activists who knowingly protect, nurture, and proliferate your employee experience and the culture that fuels it.

As a minimum, your external audience needs to be given enough information to both rationally and emotionally evaluate whether they could find a sense of belonging and value being part of what you're presenting to them. You must be able to compel the right people to act and with that very same message, repel those who wouldn't thrive or find value and meaning as part of your team.

The difference between good and world class is your ability to effectively wield the power of story.

Story is the most essential gift we can give to an employer brand—to communicate it, to breathe personality into it, and to make an emotional connection with an audience. Story is how we make sense of the world; it's how we make decisions and rationalize what's happening all around us.

Without story, the most you have is the ability to get the attention of your audience for the right reasons. Without story, we would argue, you do not have an employer brand capable of doing its job.

SUMMARY

A world-class employer brand gives you the power to recruit willing advocates, ambassadors, and brand activists who knowingly protect, nurture, and proliferate your employee experience and the culture that fuels it.

Story is the most essential gift we can give to an employer brand—to communicate it, to breathe personality into it, and to make an emotional connection with an audience. Story is how we make sense of the world; it's how we make decisions and rationalize what's happening all around us.

In the next chapter, we'll cover the essential elements of an employer brand story including empathy, affinity, change, and conflict so you can start to see how you too can craft meaningful employer brand stories.

ESSENTIAL BUILDING BLOCKS FOR AN EMPLOYER BRAND STORY

EMPATHY, AFFINITY, CHANGE, AND CONFLICT

"The purpose of a storyteller is not to tell you how to think but to give you questions to think upon."

—BRANDON SANDERSON

EMPATHY

Bryan interviewed Seth Godin, arguably the greatest marketing brain that's ever existed. He's also one of the best storytellers we've ever encountered because he goes to extreme lengths to know, understand, and empathize with his audience. He leaves no doubt that he completely understands and identifies with what it feels like to be the audience in the situation he's describing, and so when he's offering guidance, we're willing to listen.

Empathy for the audience is the most essential ingredient to the story. Without it, you have nothing.

When I (Bryan) asked Seth Godin who he thought demonstrated the most effective and powerful example of empathy within storytelling, without missing a beat he said, "Mothers." Seth explained that mothers have so much unconditional love for their children that when they communicate with their children, they do so with the most incredible empathy for how they're feeling and what they're thinking.

Mothers use empathy more than most because they love their audience (children) more than anyone else. Mothers naturally see the world through their children's eyes and use what they see to protect, educate, and nurture them. They live an empathetic life of caring that helps to create a special bond between mother and child.

One of the first books I (Bryan) read about story was *Save the Cat* by Blake Snyder, which walks you through an incredible story structure. The golden rule is to have your protagonist do something to demonstrate that they have a strong redeeming feature to their personality. Even the meanest, toughest, roughest hero types need to give us a glimpse into their hearts and their good nature if we're going to root for them throughout the story. Otherwise, as the audience, we struggle to identify with them and we don't emotionally engage. Creating empathy is everything. Snyder calls it "saving a cat," but the act of good can be anything relevant to the character or hero in your story.

AFFINITY

When crafting a story, eliciting emotion is the only game in town. Meaning produces emotion, so we must know why we're telling the story in the first place to elicit an emotional response. If we can align the meaning of the story with a primary motivator or driver of our audience, we earn their attention and create empathy and possible affinity.

For employer brand purposes, we want to put the audience to a decision after we've created empathy. Does this empathy lead to an affinity between what our employer brand stands for and what our audience believes in?

This is the magical moment where we polarize our external audience and galvanize our internal audience with the same story. We create affinity and compel the few toward our brand while we simultaneously repel the many because despite creating empathy, our audience decides they don't have what it takes or they're not willing to make the sacrifice or commitment it takes to thrive in the environment we've put on display.

CHANGE

To keep people's attention, our audience needs to see change. We want to witness our hero experiencing something new, learning and growing such that they have a different outlook on life afterward. The change can literally unfold in front of the audience's eyes, or it can be recounted to them in an engaging way and achieve the same result.

The opportunity is to tell stories whereby our meaning aligns with the change we see in front of us. This is what makes it a purpose told story.

Evidence of change is a powerful and crucial ingredient. Without it, it's just a chance to passively glimpse into a window of your company and see what it looks like but not how it feels and not what's possible within.

CONFLICT

The level of engagement to your story is directly proportional to the drama attached to the answers to these questions:

- How tough was it to learn the lesson at the time?
- What was at risk?
- What was the adversity faced?

If the change is easy and obvious, it's not very engaging. In fact, it's not interesting and it's not a true story; it's a linear narrative with limited impact.

Without conflict, there is no story. It's impossible to engage an audience on a primal, basic, human level without adopting the *Give and Get* principles of leaning into the harsh realities, vulnerabilities, and gaps in your employee experience. Once this is accepted, understood, and embraced, these perceived weaknesses start to emerge as your key differentiators—your unique opportunities and quite possibly your superpower to find people who are perfect for your organization from a cultural perspective.

If you can deliberately answer the questions about meaning, change, and conflict, you have the necessary building blocks for a compelling purpose told story that is invaluable to an audience trying to decide their future based on behavior and culture match.

If your audience empathizes with our story hero to the point where they find an affinity because of an understanding of what they want to achieve, the rest is simple. Does the audience want our hero to get what they want? If the answer is yes, then we have successfully created an affinity with the audience, and our purpose told story has just become a very valuable asset to our employer brand and EVP.

EXAMPLE: PEOPLE LIKE PAUL

Ph.Creative filmed a short story for Virgin Media, and the premise was simple—you can teach an engineer to fit a TiVo box, but you can't teach someone to care. Virgin wanted to communicate that they valued your character more than the skills you might have.

To make this point, Ph.Creative created a story where the values of our hero were put into question to give him the chance to exhibit his personal values under stress (when true values of a person are revealed).

By showing a journey unfold before us, we allowed the audience to quickly empathize with our hero and his situation; we, in turn, imagine ourselves in the same situation and are satisfied by the heartwarming outcome. The key message was received loud and clear: doing the right thing, with compassion and caring, is what Virgin values most from their employees.

The best part about this story was that it's true. The team at Ph.Creative simply applied story principles and structure to create a story with maximum impact. The campaign #PeopleLikePaul created an audience willing to listen to more information about Virgin Media.

Watch the film here: https://www.recklesskidfilms.com/.

Let's look at the building blocks, one by one:

- The **"save the cat"** moment (empathy): Paul shows he cares about Patrick when he explains he's going to be alone at Christmas.
- **The conflict:** The problem Patrick has with his TV is not Paul or Virgin Media's responsibility, yet Paul still feels responsible to help Patrick so that he's got a TV to watch over the holidays.
- **The adversity:** Paul wants to help Patrick, yet he's got a list of things to do for his wife and family if his own Christmas is going to go according to plan. He's running out of time.
- **The risk:** Paul spends his own money to go above and beyond and help Patrick. Paul might not get his money back and he might run out of time to get all his Christmas shopping done on time.
- **The change:** Paul goes from a person who feels bad about Patrick's predicament yet sticks to the parameters of his job to a man who can't live with the guilt and leaving Patrick high and dry. So he does the right thing and visibly feels good about his generous decision.
- **The values:** Paul shows empathy, compassion, support, and generosity toward Patrick.
- **The resolution:** Patrick is lost for words when Paul returns with a brand-new TV. The audience empathizes with Paul. We are proud of Paul for doing the

right thing, and the change we witness in Paul is a value we can recognize in ourselves.

Our only regret with this campaign was that we didn't consider the diversity more. The true story was in fact about two white men, but we should have taken a creative license to use underrepresented team members to break the stereotype of engineers all being men.

It's always interesting to look back and reflect on how you can improve your work and apply those learnings to your next project.

With that lesson in mind, the next year, Ph.Creative wrote a story for Continental called *Rewriting Mobility*. We used a female lead to tell the story of an engineer helping her son with a school project to demonstrate an array of employer brand messages including a passion for innovation, investing in the future safety of our roads, and work-life balance.

The two-minute story became the most viewed employer brand film in the history of Continental with over a quarter of a million total views and counting.

Watch it here: https://www.recklesskidfilms.com/.

SUMMARY

In summary, the essential building blocks for an employer brand story are:

- Empathy
- Affinity
- Change
- Conflict

#PeopleLikePaul and the Continental story are two great brand story examples you can study to see how Ph.Creative applied these ingredients to write a story that helped a megabrand achieve their employer brand goals.

In the next chapter, we'll show you how to use these same story mechanics within your employer brand essence—an overarching positioning statement that serves as an accurate depiction of the intent and reality of the employee experience. It is a compelling, single idea that provides focus for creative expression and alignment to the corporate brand and the values at the core of the organization, too.

HOW TO USE STORY MECHANICS WITHIN YOUR EMPLOYER BRAND ESSENCE

"Think before you speak and influence because your words will plant the seed of either success or failure in the mind of another."

—NAPOLEON HILL

With your employer brand essence, you don't have the luxury to spend time with your audience to tell them a fully articulated story, but you can still tell a powerful story.

Here, we're trying to pique interest, convey a point of view or a unique difference, and communicate what could be the start of a conversation found at the heart of your employee experience. That's a lot to ask from something that might turn out to be just three or four words long.

We often tackle the brand essence last because you need to be able to *see* and *feel* the entire story before you can start to craft these important words. You can't distill something down or sum something up until you have the entire story in front of you.

Have you ever written a speech and then practiced it repeatedly until you can condense it down to where you're left with just a few trigger words that can be mentally unpacked again into everything you want to say? You can apply the same technique when you are working on your employer brand essence.

The way to test your employer brand essence is to see if there is room for interruption. If it's taken literally and there's no other interpretation to be found, then it's probably not working hard enough or capturing everything you want to say.

Our brain reacts emotionally ten times faster than we create rational thoughts, which means if we get the words of the brand essence right, our audience *feels* first, but that feeling can grow and change as the words settle in. When you choose words that have multiple interpretations, we force the audience to *think* as well.

If we resonate emotionally, immediately pique interest, and solicit curiosity, then we have started to successfully engage their imagination, and this becomes infinitely more powerful if we leave space for them to fill in some vital blanks.

A lot of times, the best way to achieve this simple level of engagement is to tell only half a story and provoke the audience to complete the story for themselves based on the context of their lives.

For example, the famous Nike slogan "Just Do It" is filled with determination and has a strong call to action. However, the story is only half told because the "it" is left to the audience to decide what it means. Because of this, it's relevant to everyone who wants to embrace the sentiment, achieve more in their lives, or maintain a lifestyle. The audience finishes the story with how they see their own personal story ending. "Just do it" could mean anything from winning a competitive race, to starting to lose weight, or getting healthy for the first time in years.

EMPLOYER BRAND ESSENCE EXAMPLES
BLIZZARD ENTERTAINMENT

At Blizzard Entertainment, the secret sauce to their employee experience is centered on how special the people who work there are and what they all have in common. Ph.Creative discovered they are all obsessed with *something* they're passionate about, and whatever it is, no matter how obscure or different, it is accepted, protected, and celebrated in the most naturally inclusive manner. Blizzard is filled with different, passionate people who geek out on lots of weird and wonderful things. It's these differences that bind everyone together. Rather than not fitting in, Blizzard is a place where you belong because you're different, and that one intangible sense of belonging is what defines them. With this in mind, "Find Your People" was born.

Find Your People

"Find" suggests everyone is looking for a place to fit in, which on some level is right for all of us; however, it resonates more for people who feel like they don't fit in.

"Your" speaks directly to an internal audience member just the same as an external audience on a one-to-one level, and as a pronoun, it's very inclusive. Internally, the call to action reflects the ability to transition and try different things. It reminds us of how special the people around us really are and just how important it is to be a good member of this community.

"People" suggests the tribal nature of Blizzard and a deep sense of being human and real. By positioning the people front and center, it shows everyone just how important caring and respecting people are to Blizzard Entertainment.

Finally, the three words together let the audience imagine or recall who their people are, and it takes your imagination to a place where you can start to feel what it's like to belong—that's exactly the conversation we want to start every time someone reads the words *Find Your People*. It's the perfect place to start when we want to draw people in and then help them decide could they find their people at Blizzard or not with the Give and Get of the EVP to follow.

VF CORPORATION

VF Corporation is one of the world's largest apparel, footwear, and accessories companies. The company owns a portfolio of iconic global brands including Vans®, The North Face®, Timberland®, and Dickies®.

In working with VF, Ph.Creative discovered the 120-year-old company's greatest strength: its sheer size, heritage, experience, and maturity in the marketplace combined with a focused determination to do the right thing in the retail textile industry in a way that positively impacts the lives of people and the planet.

The sentiment of this can be replicated by many rival competitors large and small, but the global capability and influence can't. VF has 50,000 employees and business operations spanning more than 170 countries. Its global supply chain produces more than one million units of product every single day. When VF decides to improve how something is done, the entire global apparel and foot-wear industries feel it.

There are many outdoor brands and manufacturers that are idealistically focused on changing the world for the better, but VF has a bias for action rather than simply *aspiring* to make a difference. The company and its entire portfolio of twenty brands are the real deal when it comes to protecting the earth and enabling people to live active and sustainable lifestyles.

VF is filled with people who believe in the pursuit of helping others lead healthier, more fulfilling lifestyles. What binds them together is their focus on doing the right thing at scale, whatever it takes. Quite often, this means working crazy hours, demanding the best from yourself, and putting others before yourself. This environment demands a lot from everyone, and to cope and thrive there, you must love what you do on such a level that VF and the brands they stand for become part of your identity.

The employer brand essence for VF became:

Limit Less: Blur the line between a career and a calling

"Limit Less" speaks to the size and experience of VF and their structure that provides an unrivaled ability to focus on what you're there to do, without interference or distraction. It dials straight into the innate belief of thinking bigger and leveraging their capability to scale new heights, disrupt, and lead the market rather than follow. At VF, you can think bigger and have a distinct ability to bring your ideas to reality.

"Blur the line between a career and a calling" is a little long-winded for a brand essence. However, after kicking it around for weeks, testing it on the VF team on six continents in fourteen languages, we'd nailed the sentiment of passionate, commitment, and a love for the outdoors lifestyle VF was fueling at all costs. The was a big Give in that if you don't love what you do, it's unlikely the payoff is worth the sacrifice of the sometimes-long hours, challenging work-life balance, lean teams, and high expectations. We found countless stories of people doing what they do for the love of the challenge, how the subculture of a brand's lifestyle seemed to imprint on people to such a degree that it was part of who they were as teams and individuals.

SUMMARY

Our advice is to work on the brand essence last because you need to be able to *see* and *feel* the entire story before you can start to craft a few simple words that have the power to imprint on your audience. And that's a big ask, so the next chapter covers the how behind crafting a winning employer brand essence.

CRAFTING YOUR EMPLOYER BRAND ESSENCE

———

"I can't change the direction of the wind, but I can adjust my sails to always reach my destination."

—JAMES DEAN

When crafting your employer brand essence, start by thinking about the questions, assumptions, or conclusions you want the audience to arrive at. This should be driven by the overarching strength, sentiment, or unique superpower of your organization.

Once you are clear on this, brainstorm how to pique interest and start a conversation in your audience's mind. What conversation would you love to create with your audience? To get your brainstorm started, write something under each of the following headings:

- Ask a question: Why settle for less?
- Answer a question: Because here you can...

- Suggest: Why not aim higher?
- Demand something: Bring everything you've got
- Assume something: You can find it here
- Stand for something: Together, we will...

Now reflect on the personality, character, and differentiated strengths, benefits, and opportunities that your workforce holds dear. What language keeps rising to the surface? What messages need to be communicated together? What sentiment behind your brand pillars must be included? What pronouns can be used to leave an audience with open-ended space to explore? What visual language can be introduced to give the words you're crafting a precise, different, or double meaning?

If what you come up with is literal, it's good, but it's vanilla, so it's only a place to start. Dig deeper, work harder, think more creatively until you're sure you are making your audience think, feel, imagine, question, assume, or explore the questions you've asked, the story you've started, or the picture you've painted.

SUMMARY

We wish there was more of a formula to crafting the brand essence. It's more of an art than a science, and your inspiration will come from being immersed in the research, from experiencing the organization firsthand and feeling it for yourself.

Use the questions here to guide you as you embark on this important task.

Once your employer brand essence is complete, you can start on the employer brand story itself. In the next chapter, we teach you the best "beginner techniques" to get you thinking in story form and some basic structures to ensure you will be able to create compelling human stories.

HOW TO USE STORY ARCHITECTURE TO BUILD YOUR EMPLOYER BRAND STORY

———

"It is by going down into the abyss that we recover the treasures of life. Where you stumble, there lies your treasure."

—JOSEPH CAMPBELL

There are countless story structures and mechanics. What we're about to share are the best "beginner techniques" to get you thinking in story form and some basic structures to ensure you will be able to create compelling human stories.

The art of the story is just like a painting. We're going to give you some techniques, but it doesn't mean there aren't other, better ways to tell your stories. If we taught you to paint like an impressionist, pointillist, cubist, or surrealist, obviously that doesn't mean you've learned everything there is to know about art. Similarly, learning these techniques simply means you've got a place to start to begin appreciating the power of storytelling. With that in mind, let's look at some different techniques and some recommendations of where and how best to use them.

In this chapter, we will cover these four techniques:

1. Hero's Journey
2. And, But, Therefore
3. Feel, Felt, Found
4. Empathy, Curiosity, Surprise, Insight, Action

JOSEPH CAMPBELL'S HERO'S JOURNEY

This story architecture is the most complex of story structures we'll cover. It's designed to tell longer form employer brand stories with multiple characters. It's ideal for an overarching employer brand story that leans into heritage, challenges, adversity, and lessons learned.

We talked a bit about the hero's journey and its prevalence in modern-day movies earlier in the book. To recap, in these stories a reluctant hero is thrust toward a great adventure. Spurred on by a mentor character, the hero is given some form of magic and is encouraged to live out their values in a decisive crisis that puts the hero to an ultimate test. The hero, against all odds, wins a victory in the face of their biggest fears before returning home changed or transformed, helping to heal the world and restore order.

We listen to these stories because they help us believe we can be heroes in our own lives. They help us remember that the most important thing in the world isn't getting rich, finding more convenience, or a better product; it's making a difference in our communities and the world around us.

The key to using this story structure effectively for employer branding is to resist positioning the brand as the hero. Instead, the organization must take the role of the mentor/guide and tell the story of the employee experience, the change, challenge, and adversity must be experienced by the employee. The employee is the hero. This helps your internal and external audience identify and empathize with a character in a situation and career path that they very well might be in themselves.

EXERCISE

Fill in the blanks to this hero journey story structure with an employee story that you are familiar with at your organization.

Call to Adventure!

KNOWN WORLD

UNKNOWN WORLD

The Hero's Journey

Return

Threshold Guardian

Threshold

Helper

Atonement

Mentor

Challenges

REVELATION

Transformation

Temptation

Abyss Death and Rebirth

- **Explain the hero's background.** All worthwhile journeys began with an interesting setting. Describe your hero's backstory, where they've been, where they are now, and where they're headed.
- **Reveal the hero's character.** Include their strengths, flaws, weaknesses, and fears.
- **What's possible?** What does the hero hope to achieve? This endeavor must be ambitious enough to capture the imagination of the audience and compelling enough to

believably be worth the pursuit. What do they stand to gain and what's at risk if it all goes wrong?

- **The call to adventure.** What event triggers or even forces our hero into action? Usually, this inciting incident is unexpected or out of the hero's control and so forces our hero to act.

- **What adversity and conflict does our hero face?** Describe the forces working against the hero, the harsh realities and obstacles they face, and what internal demons or fears are raising their ugly head to put doubt and fear into the mind of our hero.

- **Enter the guide.** How does your brand show up to lend support? Is it in the form of a boss, a belief, a guiding brand principle or resource, or unique benefit or strength your company has to offer?

- **The trials and tribulations.** Show us what the learning journey is really like and how the hero digs deep to overcome challenges. This is the opportunity for you to reveal what values and behaviors are required to thrive within your organization. The key to this step is to be vulnerable, sharing how it can sometimes get worse before it gets better. Share the full extent of a struggle because it's directly proportional to the value of the glory and the value of the success that's about to follow.

- **Worthwhile success.** Tell the audience what it takes to win, how our hero overcomes the challenges to achieve genuine success. Typically, the value of this step is to reveal a surprise outcome over and above what our hero thought they wanted to achieve in the outset. What else did they learn and become because of the trials and tribulations of their journey?

- **The moral of the story.** Explicitly or implicitly reveal the universal truth found in your story that connects your audience to the hero with their shared values.
- **More evidence.** Use this climax to suggest or showcase other similar stories that prove that more employees have experienced a similar journey. Think about serializing your stories to engage your audience with more of the same. You might reveal different stories that focus on a different brand pillar or similar stories with different employee personas.

At this stage, purpose stories come in all different shapes and sizes, and they must be matched to the outcome you're looking for. There's no sense in using a sledgehammer to crack a nut; you don't need an epic tale to make a small point.

Further, to tell a story of grit and determination, or overcoming adversity to achieve something special does not have to be a huge drama of epic proportions. In fact, quite often the smaller the story, the better. If you can home in on something small and seemingly inconsequential to the organization that just so happened to be important to one person, consider the message you're conveying to your entire audience. The small things matter. We take notice.

We care. Not only that, but doesn't it make sense that a larger proportion of your audience will be able to identify with a smaller example of bravery or courage or innovation or gratitude than if it was a huge tale of incredible grit and determination at an extreme end of a spectrum that most people could admire but not empathize with?

I (Bryan) once spoke to an employee named Suzanne on her first day. She was shadowing a member of her new team who was taking part in a persona workshop we were running that day. It was just after lunch and I was making conversation with her as people were filtering back in to start the last workshop of the day—senior executives.

She happened to mention how much she was enjoying her first day, although she had had to find her own way to the cafeteria and ate lunch alone because her "buddy" had to leave the office for the lunch hour. She told me, "I was nervous coming in today. It felt like the first day of school. Dan has been nice. He's introduced me to lots of people already, but I can't remember anyone's name and it's a bit overwhelming." She was talking fast, nervous but excited.

She went on to say that a lovely woman ended up sitting next to her at lunch, and she told me, "I can't believe how nice the people are. They told me everyone who works here is very down to earth and friendly, but I've been amazed at how true that is. I told the woman who sat next to me at lunch how nervous I am about making a good impression—I don't feel worthy or capable at all. She gave me great advice and took my email address so she could follow up with some things that helped her on her first day. Even if she doesn't send me anything, it was nice to talk to someone who had the same fears and worries as me when she started."

In the senior executive persona session that followed, we had already identified some key themes from our wider research and we wanted to make sure resonated and to see what they meant to this group.

Inclusivity and respect were big themes running throughout the organization.

I wish I had a camera to capture the moment when the CEO of the company walked into the persona session. Suzanne's mouth dropped open, and her face turned a lovely shade of pink.

The lady at lunch was the new CEO of the multimillion-dollar company. Priceless.

This story of inclusivity and respect revolved around a brief conversation over lunch.

To Suzanne, once she got over her knee-jerk impulse to

die of embarrassment, it was everything. "OMG, the CEO of the company sat next to me at lunch and struck up a conversation. I told her all my fears and worries, and her reaction was to help me and reassure me because she had felt the same way on her first day. Amazing," said Suzanne afterward.

If you think (or read) back to the first two chapters when we look at the fundamental elements of emotions, motivators, and drivers, you will remember that purpose, impact, and belonging are at the heart of your employer brand. Why? Because that's what's most important to all of us. The seemingly small things can often matter the most.

It's not the size of the story or the enormity of the action, reaction, outcome, or resolution; it's how you make people feel that counts. Can you imagine how Suzanne felt? Can you imagine what she said over dinner after her first day in her new job? I like to think that Suzanne immediately felt a sense of belonging and a determination to create impact and purpose.

Incidentally, the CEO did send Suzanne her own hundred-day plan with notes attached for her, along with a book and two further audiobook recommendations.

Your job is to find a dozen stories like Suzanne's experience to bring your EVP to life. And remember, they don't have to be epic; they just must demonstrate the pillars of your brand.

I (Charlotte) hired a copywriting intern in the summer of 2018, the amazing Nora McNulty at UCLA, and together we wrote twenty employee stories to support the activation of Magellan's employer brand. Read them on the Life@Magellan Blog for more inspiration: https://careers.magellanhealth.com/life-magellan/. At the time of launch, the average session duration of a blog article was 3:30 minutes, showing how valuable they were to our audience.

AND, BUT, THEREFORE

This story technique is the simplest to use and the most valuable means of bringing your brand pillars to life by storifying each value exchange found within the pillar to a Give and a Get.

In 2015, I (Bryan) sat down to interview Randy Olson, a scientist, filmmaker, and author of *Houston, We Have a Narrative*, a book about story structure that he felt could deeply benefit the world of science.

Atop the cliffs looking out over Miami beach, in his home, Randy told me how he developed the And, But, Therefore (ABT) story technique based on none other than Trey Parker, writer of *South Park*.

Trey Parker writes every episode of *South Park* as quickly as he can, in a stream of consciousness. Once he's done, he goes back over the plot in the script, looks for the word *and* and tries to change it to either a *but* or a *therefore*. The theory goes that if you write something without a strong *and*, you're missing out on creating conflict and resolution.

ABT is the most concise and densely packed story structure in the world. Each ABT presents an act of the story, so it's the easiest way to introduce an act into any story, while also ensuring it encompasses the vital components to qualify as a story.

- **And** represents thesis: present, regular state
- **But** represents antithesis: change and conflict
- **Therefore** represents synthesis: resolution

Let's look at an example of how a well-known story can be reduced to a linear narrative by removing the conflict and resolution by just using *and*.

There was a boastful hare **and**

There was a slow tortoise who challenged the hare to a race **and**

The hare ran so fast that he left the tortoise far, far behind **and**

The hare fell asleep under a tree **and**

The tortoise kept on plodding along, slow and steady **and**

The tortoise won the race.

This is a narrative. Because there's no conflict or consequence established, it's just a linear description of the event. There's no story.

Now let's add the *but* and *therefore* to see what difference it makes:

There was a boastful hare **and**

There was a slow tortoise who challenged the hare to a race **and**

The hare ran so fast that he left the tortoise far, far behind

But the hare fell asleep under a tree

Therefore, the tortoise kept on plodding along, slow and steady **and**

The tortoise won the race.

Here, we see the addition of the word *but* punctuates where it all started to go wrong for the hare, suggesting he ran too fast for his own good, which meant he became tired or complacent enough to take a nap. The *therefore* links this action with the consequence of the tortoise being able to eventually win and positions the outcome as the resolution.

It seems like a tiny tweak and subtle addition of a couple of words; however, without this structural change, there's no point to the initial narrative. In the second version, now that each line is intrinsically linked to the next by consequence, there is a moral to be found—slow and steady wins the race!

If we apply that technique to an employer brand pillar, once we know we have all the building blocks of the employee experience, it becomes a powerful means of creating a meaningful *Give and Get*.

To create a clear EVP for each employer brand pillar, it's important to spell out the value exchange and the intrinsically linked *Give and Get* with credible consequence between what's expected from an employee and what they stand to gain. Essentially, we want to be able to illustrate:

- What the employee experience is really like
- What it takes to both survive and thrive
- What's possible if you're willing to put in the effort, work, sacrifice, learning, or commitment

THE BUILDING BLOCKS OF A *GIVE AND GET* EVP IN THE ABT FORMAT

PILLAR NAME	PILLAR DESCRIPTION
And	Belong: Supportive realities/upside of belonging
Thesis: Status Quo	Buy In: Purpose and vision of the company
	Benefits: Benefits, perks, and strengths of the employee experience
But	Belong: Harsh realities/challenges of belonging
Antithesis: Conflict, Adversity	Competencies: The skills, experience, and knowledge you need to have to cope
Therefore	Opportunities
Synthesis: Resolution	Personal purpose
	Impact
	Belonging

For each pillar in your employer brand, it is highly unlikely to find examples of all the building blocks in each of these boxes. However, if you can break a pillar down into all its component parts and organize them into the relevant ABT boxes, you're more than halfway toward articulating your pillar EVP in a compelling story format.

Let's look at a real example of an employer brand pillar from a Ph.Creative client, GVC.

GVC Holdings PLC is one of the world's largest gambling and online gaming companies in the world. They drive revenues of more than $3 billion a year from multiple brands, divisions, and subdivisions operating in both business-to-business and business-to-consumer marketplaces.

The pillar we'll use for our example is "Keep It Real":

KEEP IT REAL	**Give**: Bring your character
	Get: You can just be yourself

With this pillar, the *Give and Get* is clear: you must be a certain type of person to be a good cultural match into this business environment; however, it's down to earth and inclusive.

The purpose of this pillar is to both inform/remind the audience of what values and behaviors are expected culturally, as well as what's not tolerated. These are the basic table stakes required to feel like you belong. This premise is also used to reinforce the benefits of such an expectation in the form of the inclusivity that the down-to-earth vibe provides as well as the strong sense of belonging you will feel if you're able to be yourself and keep it real.

This approach to an EVP reminds us that we're both guardians and beneficiaries of the culture, and the story of the pillar highlights the opportunities this environment presents.

Let's look at the pillar with all the building blocks placed into the right ABT boxes.

Note: Not all building blocks are addressed or required for this pillar. Therefore, you have more than one pillar in your employer brand. When you look across all pillars, you should see all your building blocks used somewhere as well as your *Ikigai* being represented equally also.

KEEP IT REAL	PILLAR BUILDING BLOCKS
AND THESIS: STATUS QUO	**Belong:** Honest, down to earth, humble, you can speak your mind safely **Buy In:** **Benefits:** No bureaucracy or red tape
BUT ANTITHESIS: CONFLICT, ADVERSITY	**Belong:** If you have a strong opinion, you need to be able to back it up with evidence or action. Say what you do and do what you say in a very straightforward way. You must be willing to inclusively listen and collaborate with others. You need a strong character to cope with outspoken people. Big egos aren't tolerated by anyone. Politics or bullshit is called out quickly by everyone. **Competencies:** You need confidence in your own abilities. You must be willing to back up ideas with effort and hard work.
THEREFORE SYNTHESIS: RESOLUTION	**Opportunities:** Speak your mind and be heard. **Personal Purpose:** **Impact:** Easy to get things done quickly. Safe place to fail allows you to explore, experiment, learn, and grow. **Belonging:** It's a fun and lighthearted culture. Relaxed, informal, down-to-earth atmosphere. Diversity is encouraged, which has bred natural inclusivity, so you can just be yourself.

GIVE: BRING YOUR CHARACTER	And
GET: YOU CAN JUST BE YOURSELF	Our culture is as real as it gets. We're an honest, down-to-earth, and humble bunch, which creates a relaxed and informal atmosphere where everyone can truly be themselves.
	But
	We don't believe in bureaucracy or red tape, so we're able to work quickly and get things done.
	Therefore
	This allows our people to speak their minds, work through challenges and try something new, all without fear of failure or reproach. By joining together in these shared experiences, we create a culture that values everyone and always says, "Just be you."

FEEL, FELT, FOUND

The method Feel, Felt, Found is especially good at moving you from the past, to present, and on to a prospective future state by focusing on how people's feelings change over time.

Originating from NLP (neurolinguistic programming), the technique of Feel, Felt, Found has been most notably used in sales environments to convince customers to buy something based on a premise using social proof of previous happy customers being satisfied with their own purchase decision.

We've adapted the basic NLP principle to create a simple, yet powerful, story technique you can use to ensure you're showcasing both the Give and the Get.

Remember, change is incredibly important to tell a powerful story, and when it comes to a personal story designed to create empathy and affinity with a segment of your audience, using emotions and feelings as the main driver helps to illustrate what it feels like to work in that part of the organization.

For persona stories, often the purpose is to demonstrate examples of individual growth. Sometimes that growth/ change will be a learning experience or a simple mindset shift such as initial perception versus reality of the employee experience.

HOW FEEL, FELT, FOUND WORKS FOR PERSONA STORIES

Feel: *"I know how you feel."* The premise is designed to provide empathy with the audience by addressing a real concern, worry, or question up front to demonstrate understanding, caring, and relevance. Notice it is using the present tense.

Felt: *"I felt the same as you."* This middle component is designed to show the audience that what they're feeling is normal because others before them have felt the same. This relaxes the audience and offers a certain amount of comfort and even familiarity, depending on how the story unfolds. Notice it is using the past tense, which is a simple but effective means of linking the audience's present state with the storyteller's past.

Found: *"What I found was…"* The final resolution part of the story reveals a new discovery and how that changed how the storyteller felt as a result. Notice it is using past tense again, but this time it links the storyteller's experience with the likely future experience of the audience, thereby completing the audience's journey through time.

FEEL, FELT, FOUND EXAMPLE

Imagine a software engineer (persona) being interviewed about their early experience of joining a company and a new team. The interview is to be used as a minute video on a job description page so that candidates can get a sense of what to expect if they were to join this company.

> Intro Question: Who are you and how long have you been with company X?

> "I'm Sarah. I've been a software engineer here for nearly two years now."

> Feel Question: How does it feel to start a new job, joining a new team?

> "When you start any new job, you feel nervous about

whether or not you're going to fit in, if you can be yourself, and whether people will like you for who you are."

Felt Question: How did you feel on your first day here and why?

"I felt like a fish out of water on my first day. I was thrown into a meeting and immediately asked what I thought about a particular challenge the team was facing."

Found Question: How did you find the experience? What first impression did it create for you?

"What I found was within the first five minutes, I was contributing to the team as if I'd been there for years and nobody cared. I was quite abruptly challenged a couple of times, which took me by surprise, but in a weird way, it made me feel like part of the team. Even more, when I pushed back, I got the sense of real respect and just a simple focus on what was best for the project, rather than any ego or posturing."

Summary Question: What type of person thrives in your team?

"As long as you know your stuff and you can give as good as you get, you'll enjoy the banter, the challenge, and just how quickly we get things done as a close team."

EMPATHY, CURIOSITY, SURPRISE, INSIGHT, ACTION

This story structure is perfect for grassroots communications, especially elevator pitches to job descriptions/ads.

For explanation and demonstration, we'll focus on the job advertisement seeing how most adverts in the world suck.

In e-commerce terms, your job ad is the product page that holds all the power and responsibility to either convert someone into a customer or not. In the world of online marketing, the product page is something that is split tested, measured, refined, and honed every month, week, or in some cases, every day. Yet in recruitment, often a job description is spit out of an ATS with as much of an engaging presence as the average IKEA instruction sheet minus the diagrams.

Your job description pages can create the biggest impact of all your employer brand and EVP activation efforts, holding a disproportionate amount of power over whether a visitor decides to become an applicant.

EMPATHY

We've discussed empathy quite a lot throughout this book, and the same principle applies here. Essentially, we're trying to connect with the heart. People feel ten times faster than they think, and we want to create affinity based on the emotional pull of the vision and subsequent purpose of the company.

CURIOSITY

Once an emotional connection has been established, we draw them in further by piquing their interest even more, sometimes with a question, suggestion, or statement that creates intrigue and an appetite to continue reading.

SURPRISE

Completing the emotional connection, we use the art of the unexpected to heighten the desire of the reader and open the mind to the possibility of receiving (and remembering) facts and key information about the role. The audience might well be surprised to read about transparent harsh realities and reasons not to apply here so they can start to make a more informed decision as to whether they would be a good culture match.

INSIGHT

Here, we provide the specifics of the day-to-day role in the most inclusive manner possible by sharing examples of what they might do, day to day, and examples of what skills will be most useful to the role, too. While providing this information, we can also share aspects of character and mindset required to be able to perform well under the conditions of the employee experience.

If there are already videos of existing employees doing this role, this is the section to include it.

ACTION

Here, we simply want to create a compelling call to action for the right candidate. Usually, this is achieved by circling back to the main empathy statement and making a clear link between the role and helping the company achieve the vision.

JOB AD STRUCTURE

STEP 1: EMPATHY (HEADER)

Use empathy to satisfy purpose. Use the main sentiment from your employer brand essence.	Talk about the **company** and focus on vision, strengths, and competencies.

Example:

What if your coding expertise was the only thing stopping us from curing cancer this year?

Why this works:

Empathy is immediately created with anyone who cares about curing cancer. The vision of the company is clear, and the competency of the audience is spelled out and intrinsically linked to the vision by saying, "your coding expertise."

JOB AD STRUCTURE

STEP 2: CURIOSITY (OPENING PARAGRAPH)

Use curiosity to satisfy belonging or impact.	Use the most relevant brand pillar insights that will resonate most with your audience.	Talk about the **company and team**, and focus on the **opportunities** and aspects of the culture (realities of experience).

Example:

We're committed to funding and supporting one of the world's only dedicated software engineering teams building a solution to find tailored, personal cures for cancer 100x faster than anyone thought was ever possible.

Our team is not just filled with some of the world's best programmers and systems architects, but we're also working alongside top doctors, researchers, and scientists to make incredible breakthrough discoveries together every month. Working together as a highly collaborative, demanding, and focused team, we're looking for highly skilled and dedicated technical thinkers capable of unearthing solutions under pressure with no margin for error.

Why this works:

Curiosity is piqued by the idea of suggesting they have found a way to cure cancer 100x faster than anyone else. How? The opportunity to work with the world's best peers, the impact is to achieve something incredible and the sense of belonging comes from achieving it together as a team. The description of a pressured environment with no margin for error gives us an idea of the harsh realities to be found as well as a "demanding and focused team."

STEP 3: SURPRISE (MAIN BODY OF JOB ADVERT)

Use surprise to satisfy belonging or impact.	Use the most relevant brand pillar insights that will resonate most with your audience.	Talk about the **team and role**, focus on the **benefits** and aspects of the culture (realities of experience).

Example:

Did you know that of the current 267 cures for different types of cancer, our team was responsible for 121 of them? We estimate we have already saved more than two million people's lives, but that's not enough. With the help of your expertise, we hope to increase that impact by ten times in the next two years. Therefore, we're also one of the most highly paid and revered teams, known for our work around the world.

Why this works:

A great way to be sure to surprise an audience is to reveal unknown facts, "Did you know..."

Belonging and impact are both reinforced by using "with your help" and then spelling out what's possible.

The benefits from the role are spelled out by referencing the pay and acclaim.

JOB AD STRUCTURE

STEP 4: INSIGHT (SPECIFICS OF JOB ROLE)

Use insight to satisfy impact.	Use the most relevant persona insights that will resonate most with your audience.	Talk about the **role**. Focus on the competencies.

Example:

What you could expect to be doing daily:

- Brainstorming and testing new algorithms with peers
- Collaborating with doctors, scientists, and biologists
- Writing complex code based on new theories and disruptive ideas

The type of strengths we would like you to bring include:

- Fluent coding ability in C++ and Python
- Excellent organization and attention to detail
- Excellent written and verbal communication skills to explain complicated coding in very simple terms to a diverse audience

Why this works:

The specifics of the role provide insight into what the expectations, tasks, and specific duties are, so the audience can determine if they have what it takes to thrive, which directly addresses the potential impact and specific competencies aspect.

STEP 5: ACTION (CALL TO ACTION)

Use action to satisfy purpose, impact, or belonging.	Create a tangible link between the most relevant persona insights and the main sentiment of your overall employer brand essence.	Talk about the **company and role**. Focus on **vision, strengths, opportunities, and benefits**.

Example:

Let's crack the code to cancer together:

Find your place in history here:www.companyx.com/careers.

Why this works:

A slight play on words "crack the code to cancer" galvanizes the top-level vision of curing cancer and the specific expertise of the audience (coding), and the impact is highlighted with the final call to action, "Find your place in history."

SUMMARY

As you can now see, there are countless story structures and mechanics available to support your employer brand development and activation. In this chapter, we shared four of our favorite story structures to help you create more compelling human stories.

You should now know enough to be dangerous, as they say, to experiment with the following approaches:

1. Hero's Journey
2. And, But, Therefore
3. Feel, Felt, Found
4. Empathy, Curiosity, Surprise, Insight, Action

Now that we've covered a lot of storytelling ground, tips, techniques, and advice, let's shift gears and spend some time talking about how to activate your employer brand, paying specific attention to how to activate your *Give and Get* as well.

ACTIVATING YOUR EMPLOYER BRAND

"It isn't where you came from. It's where you're going that counts."

—ELLA FITZGERALD

Activation—both internal and external. It's time to take the strong foundation of your *Give and Get* and apply it to all the touchpoints in the candidate and employee ecosystem to attract, engage, and retain top talent. Through carefully planned activation activities, your EVPs can reach and impact talent both out in the marketplace as well as within your own company.

Each audience requires its own activation plan, budget, and measurement. Your external audience has different needs depending on what phase they are in their career search. Are they actively looking for a new job? Perhaps they are not looking but open to new opportunities—what we call a passive candidate.

Strong activation plans support candidates through the

various stages of awareness and consideration. Each piece of content you create is intentionally designed to motivate someone to progress to the next step in the process. Paid media plans are designed to support your activation goals.

When it's done well, activation is magic.

Watching your *Give and Get* come to life is powerful. It's where you share your competitive differences, the reasons to believe, and the reasons you're not right for everyone. It's when you start to repel the many and attract the few. And it's where your data and measurements start to come into view, too, so you can see the impact your employer brand and EVPs are having.

We've noticed over the years that activation rarely gets the attention, budget, and consideration that it deserves. Perhaps it's because some forget to budget for activation. Or perhaps your internal communications team doesn't know what to do with an EVP, so sometimes it never gets activated internally at all. Whatever the reason, this chapter is like a good insurance plan to ensure this doesn't happen to you.

If you remember only one thing from this chapter, what we'd like it to be is this: Building an employer brand isn't enough. An employer brand framework is useless if left on a shelf. Putting your EVPs on a PowerPoint slide, annual report, or web page will never attract, engage, and retain top talent.

With that in mind, this chapter covers the parts of activation we believe essential to not only attract high-quality talent but also re-recruit your existing workforce.

OUR ACTIVATION PHILOSOPHY: HEART, HEAD, HANDS

What does it mean to activate your employer brand? Put simply, it's time to put it to work. First, we recommend putting it to the test of whether it's accepted and believed by your employee base. Most importantly, does it have the capability to galvanize, bind, and bond your employees?

Externally, does it have the power to fuel your attraction efforts to resonate more effectively with the talent that will take your organization forward?

Activation Mission:	
Repel the many, compel the few	

Why?

Internal activation goal:	Internal activation goal:
Galvanize your audience together	Polarize your audience
Remind them why they are there and why they value their employee experience so much.	Provide the realities of what to expect, including why people value it and why others might find it challenging.

How?

1. Win their Hearts.

2. Fill their Head.

3. Equip their Hands.

The concept of Heart, Head, Hands is simple. First, we must make an emotional connection with our audience. We want to make people *feel something* about our organization to make a strong connection based on values and beliefs.

STEP 1: WIN THEIR HEARTS

The success measurement of winning the hearts of your audience is affinity. Affinity has two subtly different definitions, both of which are relevant in this case: (1) A natural liking for and understanding of someone or something. (2) The biochemistry definition, which is the degree to which a substance tends to combine with another.

If our audience begins to experience a greater affinity for your organization, we have successfully achieved stage 1 of our "hearts" activation plan. For those who do not feel an affinity for our organization, they are not your audience; they are the ones we want to repel.

STEP 2: FILL THEIR HEAD

If you give everyone a warm and fuzzy feeling every time they experience your employer brand, but they don't know *why* and can't remember what you've said, it's not going to get you very far.

We want our entire organization using the same vocabulary—explaining things the same way, giving the same examples, living the same values, telling the same stories, noticing the same behaviors, and celebrating the same victories.

Filling your audience's head is simply about establishing value and relevancy with them followed by making it easy to remember.

You've already won their hearts; now your job is to give them the vocabulary to talk about it in a consistent, on-brand way. Discover how you can remain top of mind and have them start to automatically incorporate your new employer brand into their day-to-day lives.

STEP 3: EQUIP THEIR HANDS

You've won their hearts and you've got inside their heads to the point where you have buy-in, belief, and a willingness to adopt what you've created.

Now it's time to put the tools in the hands of willing disciples, advocates, and ambassadors. What good is all this positive emotion and consistent thinking if you can't physically put it to work, right?

Internally, this can mean a multitude of different tools for different tasks at hand. Everything from simple social sharing requests and recruitment referral/advocacy campaigns, to recruiters and hiring managers having newly branded assets to make their jobs easier.

Externally, the tools required include social recruiting assets for recruiters to attract people in the right way, a new careers website to start to change and control the candidate experience such that candidates can act on their compulsion to apply more quickly and easily.

Think about all the conversations, actions, and behaviors you would like to sustainably change, update, or influence and then simply consider how you can do that more effectively with an asset, resource, tool, event, video, talk, or whatever the most appropriate vehicle for change might be.

If in doubt, simply ask your audience how you can best serve them, and they will most likely tell you. In the words of Jerry Maguire, "Help me help you."

There is a standard list of employer brand tool kit assets we always recommend. However, the most effective tools in your tool kit invariably come from a response to your research, speaking to your audience, and brainstorming with a creative team, once you have clarity on the true task at hand and the answers to the question above about what you would like to sustainably change.

START WITH INTERNAL ACTIVATION

By starting internally, you get a quick and early indication if all your hard work is going to pay off. You'll see signs of success, or opportunities and requirements to make small adjustments with messages, positioning based on feedback.

If the research has been done well, there shouldn't be any major challenges waiting for you. However, there's no harm in testing with small audience samples to be sure.

A great place to start these early tests is with any employees who have helped you with your research along the way. Include them, thank them for their input, share the results, and value their feedback. Don't look now, but you're making brand ambassadors!

The trick to internal activation is understanding and organizing exactly what you're trying to achieve with your various stakeholder groups.

PRE-INTERNAL ACTIVATION SUCCESS WITH SENIOR EXECUTIVES

Buy-in

- Tell a compelling, irrefutable employer brand story.
- Demonstrate obvious relevance and value with their existing positioning and priorities.
- Show them how easy it is for them to exhibit their alignment and support.
- Ask for the support you need to carry it forward with the gravitas, priority, and the budget it requires to become sustainable.
- Evidence their behaviors and language change quickly based on what you've shared, explained, inspired, and requested.

The desired outcome of senior executive buy-in

- **Agreement** and official sign-off
- **Advocacy** and budget for your activation plan for HR and employees
- **Adoption** of your employer brand and EVPs in their leadership messaging and communications going forward internally and externally

- **Authorship** or commentary around the culture and employee experience of your organization to use for future activation

RECOMMENDED ASSETS AND TOOLS TO REACH SENIOR EXECUTIVE BUY-IN

Deliver a high-level employer brand C-suite presentation

1. Set the scene of what, why, and how the employer brand work has been crafted. The why needs to address the cultural value as well as a clear business case. Align this business case to the existing business priorities on their desks right now.
2. Share evidence of the research findings. Build up to a clear and concise snapshot of the insights distilled because of the work. Tell the story of the employer brand conception including how you listened to their direction from the start. If you can include video footage of the research process, do it. Authentic clips of employees and peers making some of the points and using some of the language you are about to reveal are incredibly powerful.
3. Walk through each brand pillar, spelling out the Give and the Get of each.
4. Take a second to compose yourself, pause for dramatic effect, and then hit next on the slide show. Reveal your employer brand essence with a strong visual representation. Confidently deliver the line and shut up. Don't say a word. Wait. Let them speak first.

5. Usually, at this point, the CEO will cut the silence in the room by making an initial comment with a varying degree of positivity. Wait. There's more. At this point, the CHRO and other C-suite will wade in with further praise. It's the best moment of the entire project cycle and a clear indication that you're about to have a lot of fun over the next twelve months.

6. Once this has been delivered, quickly follow up with an inspirational visual snapshot of future activation activity, concepts, campaigns, and ideas painting a clear picture of what's possible. The more visually stimulating and inspiring you can make this, the better. If it's accompanied by a rough timeline/project plan of how and when it can be rolled out, that is usually very much appreciated and enjoyed as well.

OK, so the preactivation buy-in has been achieved. What else are we going to need before we jump in and start activating?

AN EMPLOYER BRAND GUIDEBOOK

Your employer brand guidebook is an extended version of the executive presentation excluding the research and including examples of all the default tool kit assets you identified as essential at the start of the project. From the framework onward, everything about the new employer brand and EVPs need to be documented, narrated, explained, and illustrated in a simple format for anyone to pick up and understand easily.

Explain the makeup, structure, and philosophy behind the work followed by a guide for how it should be used.

Anyone with a role to play in activating your employer brand needs a copy of this guide.

A UNIVERSAL EMPLOYER BRAND CHEAT SHEET

This cheat sheet should be named something a little more user-friendly such as "Who We Are: Information Sheet." You decide. The purpose of this one- or two-page PDF, five-slide presentation, or digital display carousel is to simply provide an easy way for people to remember what you've told them and start to be able to refer to it, use it, memorize it, and recall it until it becomes second nature to them.

Keep it simple and include the basics:

1. The greatest hits and vital stats of the organization
2. Who we are and why we exist
3. What we stand for
4. What you can expect to find
5. What's expected from you

Primarily, this is an internal document to make the lives

of leaders, recruiters, and hiring managers easier. However, there's no reason this can't be shared more broadly to a more general employee base and even candidates.

If you have developed different personas, consider creating a variation of the cheat sheet for each persona and tailor it based on their preferences, priorities, and specifics of their *Give and Get*.

AN EMPLOYER BRAND TOOL KIT FOR RECRUITERS AND HIRING MANAGERS

Your employer brand tool kit for recruiters and hiring managers should quickly become a go-to resource library with all the answers to their basic employer brand questions and all the tools possible to make their lives easier and more effective. The assets you provide in the library should be tailored to your organization. However, below are some examples to give you some inspiration.

"When I was a corporate recruiting leader, I coached my recruiting team to say, 'This place is not for everyone' during our recruiter screens, followed by some real talk about the positives and negatives, about the challenges, culture, resources, and role expectations. This was powerful and refreshing for talent, especially the world-class technology talent we were recruiting who were used to being 'sold' by overly enthusiastic recruiters.

"Of course, to do this well, the recruiter needs to know more than what's presented in a job description. They need to know what challenges and problems they'll face, what kind of support and training is available, and what intrinsic motivators are a match. Some candidates want to walk into a job where everything is clean with a well-defined process, whereas some like something messy to fix."

—JOHN VLASTELICA, MANAGING DIRECTOR, RECRUITING TOOLBOX

An employer brand tool kit might contain:

- Up-to-date cheat sheet
- Fresh and relevant photography
- The brand story (internal and external versions)
- Case study examples of all the EVP's *Give and Get*
- Job ad intro copy
- LinkedIn profile copy
- Branded swag for events, induction, attractions, and competitions
- Communications templates for candidate experience touchpoints
- Header and account graphics for all relevant social media channels
- Social media post graphics library
- Social media post copy library
- Social media-ready video clips, photography
- Wall signage, livery, and display graphics
- Email signature templates

"A common pitfall is trying to make every asset do everything. On their own, a pamphlet, a visual system, or an employee video can't communicate all there is to know about your brand, so don't expect them to. I think of assets and initiatives like puzzle pieces that work together to paint a complete picture."

—JADE OSTNER, EMPLOYER BRAND LEAD AT TWO SIGMA

Collecting employer brand stories along the way is essential. Here is a simple matrix to help you cover the essentials.

STORY MATRIX	EVP GIVE AND GET 1	EVP GIVE AND GET 2	EVP GIVE AND GET 3	EVP GIVE AND GET 4
UNIVERSAL				
PERSONA 1				
PERSONA 2				
PERSONA 3				
PERSONA 4				

Ideally, you need a compelling, authentic story to illustrate every aspect of your employer brand's *Give and Get*. This includes a company-wide example and a persona-specific example for each one, too. Without capturing the stories as far down as persona level, you will fail to resonate effectively with each specific segment of your audience when it comes to engagement, plus you will quickly exhaust a small number of more generic stories at a brand level.

We find that the smaller persona stories are what gets

shared, commented on, and reacted to the most because of the specificity and the greater opportunity to tell a personal and human story that directly touches upon specific examples of purpose, impact, and belonging.

"I like to create content that shares the work experience through employee spotlights, hiring manager videos, intern perspectives, location, and team features. Simple changes to our career page such as incorporating the EVP across the page, creating culture content, focusing on global teams, and location pages made a big difference."

—ALEX HER, GLOBAL EMPLOYMENT EXPERIENCE
AND RECRUITMENT LEAD, INFORMATICA

EMPLOYER BRAND PHOTOGRAPHY

Without the visual assets required to tell an authentic story, you cannot expect to see significant results from your hard work. Out-of-date photography that has not been purpose shot to illustrate your new key messages is a waste of time.

Stock photography is a great big NO.

We would much rather see amateur iPhone photographs used to showcase your new employer brand than stock photography because at least it's real.

"Candidates are savvy; they know when you are using stock

images or showing them photos that reflect your people and your workspaces...or not. When we film, we ask open-ended questions, and I'm continually amazed by the answers given. They organically support our EVP. I guess that's a true test of an EVP—having your associates respond spontaneously and unsolicited with a story that you as an employer brand marketer are trying to tell."

—LIZ GELB-O'CONNOR, VICE PRESIDENT
EMPLOYER BRAND, ADP

EMPLOYER BRAND CORNERSTONE VIDEO

Creating an employer brand video is a must. You don't have to invest in big-budget production to tell a compelling story effectively. Currently, it's a requirement, not a luxury. How you produce the video is a matter of appetite, inspiration, budget, and timing usually. However, there's no better way to tell your story than through a compelling video.

This is your opportunity to create a compelling visual positioning statement for your employer brand, the EVPs, and what the employee experience really feels like.

The filming exercise itself is usually a very powerful internal activation project, and if it's executed creatively, there should be multiple edit options and uses for what you capture on screen.

During your employer branding project, also consider capturing the following footage for later use:

- Capture B roll of real employees in real working situations.
- Capture behind-the-scenes footage of anything you're doing to create the tool kit and activate the employer brand such as photo shoots, filming, workshops, and interviews.
- Capture employee stories of how each EVP makes people feel (see story chapter for practical how-to advice).
- Capture manager and leader interviews of what they expect and demand from their team, as well as what they're capable of and what they've achieved (*Give and Get*).
- Capture evidence of the organizational purpose at work.

SUMMARY

Watching your *Give and Get* come to life during activation is powerful. It's when you start to repel the many and attract the few. And it's where your data and measurements start to come into view, too, so you can see the impact your employer brand and EVPs are having.

As we said in the opening, if you remember only one thing

from this chapter, what we'd like it to be is this: Building an employer brand isn't enough. An employer brand framework is useless if left on a shelf. Putting your EVPs on a PowerPoint slide, annual report, or web page will never attract, engage, and retain top talent. Use the tactics listed in this chapter to pick the right mix of assets to help your organization attract high-quality talent and re-recruit your existing workforce.

The next chapter covers the practicalities and project management side of internal activation. It's packed with sample plans that Charlotte has used over the course of her career to great success.

THE PRACTICALITIES AND PROJECT MANAGEMENT OF INTERNAL ACTIVATION

"Just keep swimming."

—DORY

Start with a communication plan that maps out how to introduce your employer brand to your workforce. There are numerous advantages to activating internally, but the primary reason to start internally is to project a consistent and aligned message to candidates during interviews and referral inquiries. Anyone referring, interviewing, or answering questions about your company should know enough about your employer brand that they share a consistent story and have visibility into campaigns should a candidate reference them in conversation.

You don't want to appear disconnected; after all, the goal is to produce an aligned messaging system that convinces new hires to join and reminds people why they should stay. With that in mind, plan a communication cadence that covers the basics.

SAMPLE INTERNAL COMMUNICATIONS PLAN

AUDIENCE	TOPIC	VEHICLE
TA Team	Talent acquisition preview with a tool kit of new assets and training materials/schedules	Meeting
Divisions	Leader road shows	Road show
HR	HR advance, covering how they can help support activation	Email
Leaders and Hiring Managers	Leader advance with talking points	Email
TA Team	Thank the team for their support and link out to the new assets	Email
All Employees	Weekly Teasers: Begin countdown of Five Reasons to Work at...	Email Intranet Workplace
All Employees	Launch email	Email
Hiring Managers	What to expect with the new recruiting campaign	Email
All Audiences	Our new social campaigns	Social media
All Employees	Peek inside the creative work	Intranet Workplace
TA	Monday morning tip highlight an asset and how to use it. Highlight team members who are adopting the materials	Email

DRAFT ACTIVATION PLAN

We wanted to include an early-stage activation plan. Notice it's not fully developed; that's intentional to bring internal stakeholders along the journey.

Give your stakeholders a chance to incorporate their ideas, rather than give you "approval." When the final plan is a collaboration, you'll get more support, buy-in, and advocacy.

INTERNAL TALENT BRAND ACTIVATION PLAN

Goals

- Recruitment
- Talent referrals
- Passive media campaigns that drive talent community sign-ups
- Career site conversion rates
- Culture
- New hire orientation
- How we assimilate new hires
- Ongoing training programs
- Talent management life cycle
- Support requested

The more we embed the EVP into all that we do, the more it becomes part of our ethos. With the talent brand ready to go, our next step is to chart out how and when we will weave the concept into the buckets of work outlined above.

We're requesting the support and collaboration of TA, Talent Management, Wellness, and Internal Communications to build out individual project plans, timelines, and responsibilities to activate the talent brand. Once each team identifies the tactical elements needed, we will provide the creative assets, messaging, and guidance to incorporate the talent brand into each focus area.

Objectives

What we aspire to achieve as an employer:

- **To recruit from a position of strength:** Earn a reputation in the marketplace where we don't have to spend time trying to convince people why they should work for us.
- **To increase our recruiting power exponentially:** Turn our entire workforce into a team of headhunters.
- **To give our employees a coherent, compelling message to pass along:** Everyone is consistently "on message" and tells others about why Magellan is such a great employer and place to work.
- **To unleash the power of storytelling:** Seek out and leverage stories about the experiences people have with Magellan to illustrate the tangible value we bring to people's lives.
- **To transform our employees into talent magnets themselves:** Build a team that embodies our spirit and reflects our beliefs to become walking talent magnets, attracting people like themselves to the Magellan work experience.

Strategy

Coordinate a two-week internal campaign to promote and celebrate the newly created EVP before the external activation.

Tactical elements to consider:

- The campaign should kick off with an all-employee email from the project team
- Support the memo with a campaign blitz across our offices and internal comms channels
- Introduce the talent referral campaign via digital assets for email, the intranet, as well as physical posters for offices
- Internal comms team support needed to drive awareness, excitement, and engagement
- Identify brand ambassadors such as employee resource groups to help drive the campaigns and provide ground support in offices
- Train TA and hiring managers
- Identify opportunities for internal office branding

Simple Activation Ideas to Embed EVP and Talent Brand

- **Ask Us**—Leaders commit to answering any question about the employer brand on a live workplace session once a week for a month. Questions are asked and vetted in advance but answered and shared live. Or candidates can ask TA via Facebook Live, etc.
- **Nominate the best example of our employer brand in your team.** Enter them by writing a reason and uploading a picture of the

employee/hero. Winners get something personal and visible in their working environment, and the results are shared in social channels.

- **Give us your stories.** #branded hashtags are promoted via email, office posters, and short video trailers.
- **Series of one-minute stories** articulating your brand pillars in action.
- **T-shirt artwork designed** around each pillar articulating the spirit of the EVP and tailored/personalized for each persona/territory/ motivational quote, etc.
- **Branded swag**
- **Kids painting competition—"Why we love company X."** I love company X because my mommy can work from home. I love company X because they help protect the planet. Turn the pictures into wall art, company calendars, screen savers, etc.

SUMMARY

There are numerous advantages to activating internally, but the primary reason to start internally is to project a consistent and aligned message to candidates during interviews and referral inquiries.

Internal activation is a team sport. Partner with your internal communication, talent management, corporate communication, and human resource teams to plan. The sample plans in this chapter should be tailored into something that will work best for your organization.

And as you start to get deeper in thought about how to

activate internally, we want you to think about which stories, which voices are best suited to help you activate. In the next chapter, I (Charlotte) share a lesson I learned early in my career that changed the way I approached my work from that day forward: the power of a well-told story internally to re-recruit your existing workforce.

HOW TO RE-RECRUIT YOUR WORKFORCE WITH YOUR EMPLOYER BRAND ACTIVATION

"Social connection is such a basic feature of human experience that when we are deprived of it, we suffer."

—LEONARD MLODINOW

Time and time again, with our own eyes, we've seen the power of story influence employee engagement, even in tough cultures, so much so that we've written an entire chapter on it. However, I (Charlotte) learned this early in my career and I want to share this lesson with you now.

In 2010, I led employer branding, recruitment marketing, and HR communications for Life Technologies, a global biotech company that was experiencing rapid expansion from a few thousand employees to an international behemoth with more than 12,000 employees, 50,000 products, and sales in 180 different countries.

Our CEO often claimed publicly that our ability to grow was driven by our ability to attract, develop, and retain world-class people who thrived in our environment and shared in our desire to improve humankind. My focus on employer brand helped prepare the company for its acquisition by Thermo Fisher for $13.6 million, a 12 percent premium.

The campaign we created did a couple of things well. It drove down the overall cost per hire by $1,500/hire and raised the employee engagement index by seven points in two years.

Looking back, the primary driver of these results points to the use of story, real stories that featured people who benefited from our products—their photos, their voices, their real-world impacts.

I'll never forget bringing Herman Atkins in to speak to our workforce at an all-employee meeting. Two thousand people gathered in a large warehouse, and another several thousand connected via a live stream.

Our CEO always opened all-hands meetings with a joke. As employees filled the room, I remember there was a casual ease in the air as everyone knew a laugh was forthcoming.

What no one knew walking in was that this time, this

meeting was going to be different. Our CEO didn't start the meeting with a joke. Rather, he went on to say that there was nothing funny about the situation we found ourselves in that day, that quarter. We were experiencing an economic winter, and if we didn't turn things around, the company wasn't going to survive.

Silence filled the room.

During this unexpected opening, I was sitting backstage with Herman, a man who was wrongfully convicted of a crime in Los Angeles, California, in 1988, and eventually exonerated by DNA evidence twelve years later. He was eventually released, thanks to the DNA testing made possible by the team at Life Technologies.

I'll never forget when Herman took the stage. Having just heard the CEO's remarks, he took the stage and started out by saying that he didn't know much about our business and the numbers we needed to hit, but he did know that the people in this room gave him his life back.

He described the look on his mother's face when he told her about the charges. He described the heartbreak he felt when she looked at him as if she didn't believe him. He described life behind bars and how helpless he felt until DNA testing became available.

Little did anyone know, I found the data scientist who created the product used to analyze the DNA in Herman's case and flew him into Carlsbad to be at the meeting in person. After Herman told his story, we asked the scientist to join us on stage, and we watched them exchange a warm embrace.

It was a moment I'll never forget. It was the moment that started a fascination with authentic, purpose-led stories that have defined much of my career ever since I felt what sharing Herman's story did to an organization.

The next quarter, we had another special guest join our all-hands meeting—Brenda Maribel Corado. Brenda was a thirty-two-year-old mother who was walking her three-week-old baby to a doctor's appointment in Guatemala when a couple of women approached her on the street and kidnapped her daughter.

Two months passed before the baby was found. If it were not for a DNA test—a test created by Life Technologies—there would have been no proof that she was Brenda's daughter. The test result was a 99.9 percent match.

With the help of an employee translator, Brenda took the stage and told the room what it felt like to have her baby ripped from her arms. We hosted a robust dialogue around child trafficking and realized that without our products, there would not have been a happy ending in this case. Brenda's story was a reminder of the power of what we were there to do. And while we all knew deep down that our work made a difference in the world, that day we felt it as we watched a toddler sprint across the stage and babble with the crowd.

As employer brand practitioners, we have the power to make people feel—deeply.

The stories that people care about live with us. It's our job to find them. It's our duty to bring them to life. When I was working at Life Technologies, I remember thinking how odd it was that the company had so many amazing stories that had never been told.

The marketing team knew of Herman, but when I asked them why they didn't promote the story, they told me they didn't have confidence our product was used to analyze his evidence. We owned most of the market but not all of it, so there was a chance it was a competitor's DNA test, and no one wanted to take that risk.

I made one phone call—to the Innocence Project, the non-profit organization that advocated for Herman's evidence to be tested. They pulled up the case file and identified the lab that ran the analysis. Within a week, I had what we had been missing: the name of the product used. It was ours.

To find Brenda's story, I made another call. This time to DNA Pro Kids, a third party organization we partnered with to provide access to our technology in third world countries. They put me in touch with several families who benefited from our technology.

Discovering these stories changed the way I viewed my work. Every time I found a new story, it became easier to get investment to bring it to life. After all, everyone could feel the impact these stories were having on our workforce. I found myself on a fast path to promotions and bigger opportunities because there was so much value and visibility into my work.

And it got easier. The more stories we told, the more stories started to surface organically. When they surfaced, I brought them to life in a variety of ways:

- Office signage
- Floor talkers in manufacturing facilities
- Digital and print ads
- Videos

We designed a state-of-the-art candidate experience center where all our interviews were conducted in the global headquarters. These stories dressed the walls.

Two years later, engagement jumped seven points.

SUMMARY

The stories that people care about live with us. It's our job to find them. It's our duty to bring them to life. Finding the stories is the hardest part, but as they say, the juice is worth the squeeze.

The simple tips and techniques shared in this chapter will help you re-recruit your workforce. Start with a solid communication plan that includes other stakeholders and their ideas. When you cover these bases, your key metrics will improve over time.

In the next chapter, we cover another tactic to activate a newly donned employer brand: a refreshed employee referral campaign. It's highly visible, a good source of quality applicants, and can be accomplished on a small budget. Winning!

ACTIVATE WITH A REFRESHED REFERRAL CAMPAIGN

———

"I get by with a little help from my friends."

—RINGO STARR

The 2018 Candidate Experience Research Report by the Talent Board stated that 42.7 percent of referred candidates were more likely to increase their relationship with a potential employer (apply again, refer others, make purchases) than if they conducted their own search or if they received unsolicited outreach from a recruiter.

Knowing all this to be true, it's still a good idea to present a business case that stacks up to ensure you get the budget you need to build a refreshed campaign.

BENEFITS OF FOCUSING ON EMPLOYEE REFERRAL PROGRAMS (ERP)

If you are new to employer brand, take a few moments

to learn the value of employee referrals. After knowing how much value they offer your company, plan to create a campaign to promote referrals internally and watch the ROI roll in.

HIGHER CANDIDATE QUALITY

Data shows that referral candidates can be five times more likely to get hired than other candidates. This is because educated employees know that their role is to seek out individuals with superior skills and experience. And because referral candidates are proactively sought out and prescreened by your employees who know the job and the company, the candidate pool is higher quality than most sourcing pools that are made up of "active candidates" who found the firm on their own (most referrals are currently employed).

QUALITY OF HIRE

New hires from well-designed referral programs routinely produce the highest on-the-job performance of any recruiting source. In addition, referral new hires have significantly higher retention rates than hires from other sources.

CANDIDATES ARE A BETTER CULTURE ADD

Well-designed referral programs produce a high percentage of candidates who thrive within your culture. This is because your employees know your corporate culture better than anyone.

FASTER TIME TO INITIAL PRODUCTIVITY

Higher quality hires mean that new hires get up to speed faster. In addition, because many employees will mentor, guide, and assist the individuals whom they have referred, often the time to productivity will be even faster.

SUMMARY

We highly recommend that you include a referral refresh in your activation plans.

It's a good idea to work with your Talent Operations team to reduce friction or points of frustration from your actual policy before you dive into the creative exercise. Once that is complete, a few creative assets to promote the referral policy go a long way to get quality applicants in the door.

The next chapter should not be missed. One of the biggest missteps I (Charlotte) ever made came down to underestimating recruiter and hiring manager adoption of a newly designed employer brand. It's always one of the hardest parts of the process, so in the next chapter we dive into the lessons learned and key considerations you can apply to your activation strategy.

RECRUITER AND HIRING MANAGER ADOPTION

"A little consideration, little thought for others, makes all the difference."

—EEYORE

In our opinion, this is the hardest part of activation. You've spent months building a library of assets and a simplified story of who your company is and why it's worth working for. Now you must find a way to get your hiring teams to:

1. Learn the campaign
2. Familiarize themselves with your stories
3. Learn how to leverage these key messages in conversations with candidates

This is easier said than done. First, the people you need to influence are busy. The hiring managers often don't see this as a top priority, so getting their attention is a real challenge.

Knowing this, it's important that you communicate the

importance of hiring manager/recruiter education. Work with your leadership teams to drive accountability and adoption. It's unlikely at a large organization you'll succeed going at this alone. If your TA team is made up of a team of leaders, start with them. Let them know what you want/ need their teams to do and drive accountability.

Ensure the content resonates with your target audiences and is easy for them to learn and leverage. We like to share the training materials with a small test audience to get trusted feedback before deploying them.

When it comes to the content itself, show how you've articulated the *Give and Get* across your career pages, your job descriptions, and your social media promotions. Show how you're leveraging EVP as a smart filter to repel talent so that by the time they are on the phone with a recruiter, they are already prepared for the harsh realities and cultural norms we want them to buy into.

This should get them excited and engaged. If you've done persona work, showcase that as well. Here is a sample request for feedback that will make you look like a pro:

Greetings,

I am working on an employer brand strategy for our team. As a first step, I've drafted [insert description].

I'd like to test this draft with you for your trusted feedback. Please review the link below and let me know your thoughts on it as well as answers to the questions below.

[insert link]

How does this resonate with you?

Is it easily understandable?

What will the TA team struggle with, if anything?

What would you add/delete if you had to author?

Thanks for your input. Responses are appreciated by next [add date].

I ask you not to forward, as this draft is subject to modification.

SUMMARY

People trust their peers and employees more than just about anyone else. It's essential that you involve employees during activation. This chapter covered how to turn your workforce into talent magnets by arming them with the stories, passion, and permission to talk to the world about where they work—otherwise known as advocacy.

When getting started on your employee advocacy program, here are the things to keep in mind:

- Give your blessing and encourage employee participation.
- Find your stars and recognize employee advocates.
- Help employees build their personal brand.
- Create a branded hashtag.
- Create a social playbook.
- Invest in an advocacy tool.
- Draft a Glassdoor review strategy.

In the next chapter, let's explore how to apply the principles behind *Give and Get* to your career website. We'll focus in on the key opportunities to apply *Give and Get* value exchanges in the areas that drive the highest conversation opportunities.

APPLYING THE *GIVE* AND *GET* TO YOUR CAREER WEBSITE

"You get what you give."

—JENNIFER LOPEZ

Your career site is the center of the universe when it comes to your employer brand. It needs to make your candidates *feel* something.

We tend to focus on the home page when designing a website. However, if you look at the traffic coming into your site, 80 percent of candidates arrive on your site via a job board, which means they bypass your home page and jump straight into a job landing page. It's amazing how underutilized job description pages are when it comes to candidate attraction.

If you remember only one thing from this chapter, what we would like it to be is this: when designing your career site, enhance your job descriptions because they directly increase the quantity and quality of applicants.

"A lot of employer brands look the same, a sign of creative imma-
turity in my mind. Expression is all too literal, and there are
not enough ideas being used to express these brands. Push your
partners to be creative and look for ways to push the boundaries
on your career site and beyond. If you do this right, the impact
will be incredible. It will define your career and your company.
You will harness the potential waiting for us all—right here,
right now."

—STEFAN SHAW, CREATIVE DIRECTOR AT PH.CREATIVE

ENHANCED JOB DESCRIPTIONS

Shane Gray at Clinch told us a funny story that warmed
our *Give and Get* hearts:

> "Someone once asked me, what is the best possible candidate
> experience a person can have? My answer, not applying for
> the job you have no chance of getting."

Ninety-nine percent of the time, recruitment is in the
rejection business, an appalling waste of time and money
with significant human cost on both sides of the process.

One of the most impactful ways to improve this situation
is to use your employer brand and help more people self-
select out of the process before they apply.

Shane says, "As the old sales adage goes, good long copy

always outsells short copy because it leaves no question unanswered in the buyer's mind. Most job descriptions leave every question unanswered in a candidate's mind about why they should consider this employer for their next opportunity. Employer brand delivered at the right place at the right time is the secret weapon that can fill in the gaps for a candidate and engage the right people."

As candidates weigh up whether to apply to a new opportunity or accept an offer, they need to overcome the fear of not being happy there and the fear of failing there.

All candidates want to know:

1. Will I find purpose?
2. Can I make a difference?
3. Will I feel like I belong?

These questions all add up to, "Will I survive, or better yet, thrive at this organization?"

Fear of failure is a huge psychological barrier. In fact, it's the number one reason people don't set goals or try new things.

A job preview should address the real driving fears of the candidate to repel the many yet compel the few well-suited candidates toward your brand. To do this successfully and most effectively, companies must be brave enough to show candidates the truth about what's potentially lurking in their near future. What harsh realities will they encounter? What adversity will they face? What struggle will they find?

When organizations reveal the truth in all its glory, complete with showing their current heroes (existing employees, future teammates) successfully slaying those dragons and feeling proud, candidates are left feeling assured, safe in the knowledge that they can also win out in the end.

What's more, the strengths, benefits, and opportunities at your organization are now much more desirable because we know what it takes to achieve and deserve them.

Some candidates are left feeling, "The wall is too high to scale," and others, "The wall is sufficiently high enough to bring meaning and value to my climb." In both cases, they want and need to understand the size of the struggle and decide for themselves if the juice is worth the squeeze.

So let's show them.

HOW TO CREATE AN EFFECTIVE JOB PREVIEW

Try producing employee stories and consider asking the following questions:

1. What was your biggest fear before taking on your current role?
2. What's the toughest lesson you've learned about working here?
3. What has been your proudest achievement and why?
4. If it was your job to convince someone not to apply, what would you say?
5. What does it take to thrive, not just survive, here?
6. What's the biggest source of satisfaction here?
7. How does working here make you feel?

Ask follow-up questions to all those above until you can edit a story arc that resembles something like this story below. I've broken it out into three distinct parts, so you can see the structure more clearly.

Step 1: Address the real challenges and face the fears.

It can be tough here because...

I hadn't anticipated being in a role where you must...

I was afraid I couldn't cope with...at first because...

It made me feel...and my biggest fear was...

Step 2: Provide insight into how you can approach the challenges and the journey of growth and achievement you will go on.

However, what I found was…

And after learning to…and quickly getting better at…I started to enjoy it, and now I would say I'm more…

Looking back, I wish I had known…

Step 3: Affirm what it takes to be a real survivor, and reveal the value it brings in all its glory.

To do this role, you must be able to…

If you can, it's fantastic because…

The reason I'm here is…

JOB DESCRIPTION CHECKLIST

In addition to writing enhanced job descriptions, there are lots of content opportunities to wrap content around your jobs that candidates really value. Clinch has seen these job description enhancements help companies improve candidate flow by up to 400 percent. This list is ordered based on the preference of candidates when asked what information they would most like to know about a company before they apply.

Candidates want to know:

1. **Company Values.** What are the values of the organization? Summarize them and add a link to them on the job page.

2. **Company Culture.** If you have a strong culture, don't shy away from talking about it on the job page. Discerning candidates want to know if you are a match for them before they apply.

3. **Employee Testimonials.** Videos, personal blog posts, and interview snippets are a great way to showcase the people potential candidates will be working with.

4. **Product Information.** If you are a product company, people want to know about the products they are going to be building, selling, or supporting.

5. **Company Performance.** Been around for fifty years and still growing strong? Tell me that story if it will help derisk my decision to move on from my existing role.

6. **Career FAQs.** How does the application process work? How long will it take to hear from someone? The more questions you answer on the job page, the less time a recruiter will spend answering the same questions over and over when they are screening candidates.

7. **Diversity.** Talk about your diversity culture from the moment a candidate arrives at a job. Don't make them hunt out the well-hidden page on the career site. Use your people's stories to showcase the wide range of talent you value.

8. **A Picture of Their Desk.** Yes, that's right. It's amazing how much this can tell a candidate about where they will be working.

9. **A Map of the Office Location.** Let's be honest, no one is going to commute more than an hour or so. Why not make that easy to figure out up front and save a ton of wasted applications and screening effort?

10. **Similar Jobs.** Make it easy for me to search again or at least browse similar jobs. The addition of a Google-powered search bar will reduce the bounce rate by 50 percent, giving you more time to engage candidates before they leave.

Apply these tactics and see a reduction in bounce rate and improved conversion to completed applications. And the good news is that the increased flow includes more well-informed, committed candidates who go further in the rest of the hiring process and make your recruitment team's life a little easier.

LIFE@BLOG

A life@ career blog is one of the best ways to activate your EVP. We've already talked at length about the need to produce stories that show how your employees are living your brand pillars. Now you need a central place to house them.

TIPS TO GET STARTED:

- Start with five to ten blog posts that show a variety of voices and content types.
- After your stories are complete, promote the stories across your internal and external channels.
- One piece of long-form content can be used in a variety of ways. For example, say you have a library of twenty stories on your blog. You can promote the same story internally and externally.
- Encourage a variety of voices on your blog. You don't need to write them all. Ask your TA team, new associates, leaders, and more to guest write.
- We've seen better engagement when employees post their stories directly on their LinkedIn pages. Consider a linking strategy that accounts for this variance.

STORY DISTRIBUTION CHECKLIST

Your blog story is published—now what? Below are some options for sharing it with the world.

Social Media

Share the link on your company's social accounts and consider paid uplift. And ask employees to share as well. They can:

1. *Write their own post.* This is especially great if they mention not just that they like working at your company but also why.
2. *Share your post.* Once you've shared the link on your company accounts, they can retweet, share, or like your post.
3. *Update their bio.* They can link to the story right in their profile. (This is especially useful on Twitter.)

Careers and Profile Pages

Link to the story from your company's careers page and from its profile pages on LinkedIn, Glassdoor, Fairygodboss, Comparably, and so forth.

Invitations

Include a link in your announcements for events as appropriate.

Email Signatures

Include a link to the story. You may want to give them suggested copy, such as "We're hiring! Learn more about our team."

Recruiter Outreach Emails

Include a brief mention of the story as an opportunity to learn more.

Job Descriptions

Include a link and a brief description of all related job descriptions.

Candidate Emails

Share a link when scheduling interviews to offer fresh information on the team.

SUMMARY

Your career site is the center of the universe when it comes to your employer brand. It needs to make your candidates *feel* something. While a lot of this happens through bespoke design and strong user experience work, there are a few simple things everyone can do straight away to improve and activate your new employer brand on your career site.

Start with a focus on enhancing your job descriptions because they directly increase the quantity and quality of applicants, and a Life@blog to house the stories you create. Apply basic baseline metrics before and after so you can see the uptick and focus on continuous improvement.

Now that we've covered job descriptions, there are lots of other content considerations that will help you successfully activate your employer brand. In the next chapter, we'll explore how to use content to nurture talent through the key consideration stages: See, Think, Do, Delight.

For a more in-depth explanation of See, Think, Do, Delight, see Bryan's first book, *Getting Goosebumps*, which is more specifically focused on digital attraction tactics using this marketing funnel methodology.

CONTENT IS QUEEN

"Victorious warriors win first and then go to war, while defeated warriors go to war first and then seek to win."

—SUN TZU

SEE, THINK, DO, DELIGHT

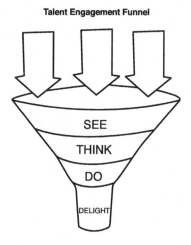

Talent Engagement Funnel

SEE

THINK

DO

DELIGHT

Attraction starts with brand awareness, which means that people need to know you to want to work with you. Your job is to create a persuasive message that grabs attention and help your personas **See** you as a potential employer.

Once you've spiked interest and have your personas engaged, you need to match your roles and experience with their needs, helping them Think "this job is ideal for me" through tactical executions.

Interested and informed, you now want your personas to Do something to build deeper engagement. Challenge and entertain them with interactive formats. Create moments that drive them to act (apply, sign up, watch a video, take a quiz, etc.).

Finally, you need to consider the application and selection process. Whether a candidate is successful or not in the process, there's a chance for you to Delight everyone who touches your brand and make them feel valued.

Now that you have a quick introduction to the types of content you need to create for activation, here is a list of content types that fall under each stage.

SEE	THINK	DO
Testimonials and quotes	Meet Your Boss Video	Chatbots
Blog: Day in the Life	360 video—workspaces	Live demonstration
SlideShares	Demo video	Meetups/events
Polls	Solution-focused white paper	Content-rich JD page
Checklist	Solution-/expert-focused webinar	Talks
Introductory eBook		Webinars
How-tos	Product spec sheet/download	Conferences
Educational webinar	FAQs download	Personality tests
Infographic	Calculator	Helpful application/tool
Podcast	Trend report	How well matched are you to our company quiz
Photos	Forum	
Guide or tutorial	Interactive blog	Remarketing
Resource roundup	Survey	Email marketing
Glossary	Live Q&A	
Interview	Infographics	
Template download	Success stories	
Predictions	Press releases	
Competition	Original research	
User-generated content	Mind maps	
Company news	Opinion post	
Meme generator	Tip sheet	
Sticky landing pages	A definitive guide for...	
Charts/graphs	Industry survey publish results then weekly discussion on results	
Timelines		
Ego jacking the industry: "Top 50 creative thinkers of 2018"	Ego jacking the industry: "Top 50 creative thinkers of 2018"	
Games	Interactive blog	
Videos that get attention	Crowdsourced challenge	

Examples of content for See, Think, Do:

	TOPIC/TITLE	CONTENT/ DETAILS	KEYWORD(S)/ SEO	OFFER/CTA
SEE	Blog series, called *Analyze This*	Podcast series featuring human stories of adversity that contributed to the business. People who have made an impact and life lessons from those people.	Think about an SEO strategy to drive traffic to a sticky landing page for that persona that drives traffic to open jobs.	Subscribe Link ideas: Series link the last three articles; twelve books every data analyst needs to read; top ten qualitative questions to ask in every survey
THINK	Invite viewers to explore the workspace via a 360-video story focusing on highlighting the working environment for our personas.	Guide viewers around a workspace and introduce them to different personas. Dive deeper into a selection of employee stories highlighting areas of interest in the environment, projects, and the people you'd be working with.		Sign up for our talent community, short-form lead capture
DO	Interactive Culture Match Quiz, "How Magellan Are You?"	Challenge candidates to put their skills to the test, create a quiz to match brand values, "How Company X Are You?"—> you are 95 percent company X. Apply now!		Apply now

SUMMARY

We hope these examples of different types of content you can create serve as inspiration for you to start to craft content ideas for each stage: See, Think, and Do. In the last phase, Delight, we focus on creating a memorable candidate experience. Let's conclude with a look at why candidate experience is a critical part of the process.

CANDIDATE EXPERIENCE

—

"People will forget what you say, people will forget what you did, but people will never forget how you made them feel."

—MAYA ANGELOU

We have a plethora of data at our fingertips proving the business impact of candidate experience. The data consistently shows that candidates who have had a negative candidate experience take their wallet and relationships somewhere else. According to the 2018 Candidate Experience Research Report, "this means a potential loss of revenue for consumer-based businesses, referral networks for all companies, and whether or not future-fit and silver-medalist candidates apply again."[4]

The groundbreaking Virgin Media candidate experience case study by Ph.Creative is a great example. If you haven't read it, Google it. The CliffsNotes version is that Ph.Creative proved £4.4 million of lost consumer revenue was

---

4   Talent Board, *2018 Talent Board North American Candidate Experience Research Report*, February 7, 2019, cited in press release: https://www.thetalentboard.org/press-releases/the-2018-talent-board-north-american-candidate-experience-benchmark-research-report-now-available/.

the result of negative candidate experiences of applicants who were also customers at the time. Fast forward a year later, they focused on candidate experience and turned TA into a massive revenue generator for Virgin Media, rather than a loss.

STATS FROM THE 2018 CANDIDATE EXPERIENCE REPORT, TALENT BOARD

Improve Candidate Engagement Pre-Application: We saw a 69 percent increase in employers utilizing chatbots on career sites in 2018. More employers realize that a competitive differentiator is communicating earlier with candidates, even before they apply. Chatbots are being used to answer general employment questions and this frees up the recruiting teams to have more hands-on time with potential candidates already in play.

A Fair and Simple Application Process: Perceived fairness continues to be a differentiator in candidate experience, and there's no better crossroads of this than at the application process. This is as far as most applicants make it today in the recruiting process, and there was a 128 percent difference between those who felt they were being treated the most fairly, 4.4 out of 5-star rating, and those who rated application fairness the lowest, just about 1 out of 5 stars. And 42.5 percent of the candidates who rated the application process 5 stars said the application took less than 15 minutes, a trend we continue to see with many companies.

Immediate Feedback Pays Off: Candidates who were interviewed and then given job-related feedback by the end of that same day said they were 52 percent more likely to increase their relationship with the employer (apply again, refer others, make purchases when applicable). Whereas, if feedback was not given, they're more than twice as likely to sever the relationship (8 percent vs. 2.6 percent). This was greater than even those who were given just recruiting process feedback at the end of the day (next steps), which still included 41 percent of candidates more likely to increase their relationship.

Let the Candidates Shine: The only way to truly know if candidates are qualified is by giving them a fair opportunity to present their skills, knowledge, and experience during the screening and interview process. Of candidates who gave a 5-star rating for the screening and interview process, 73.8 percent were extremely satisfied with their ability to do just that, while 53 percent of the candidates who rated the experience 1-star told us they were extremely dissatisfied with the screening and interview process.

Pick Up the Phone: The types of rejection communication candidates receive when they were no longer being considered after the screening and interview process can make a big difference in whether they apply again or refer others. According to our data, these included automated email replies (63 percent), personal emails from recruiters and hiring managers (21 percent), and personal phone calls from recruiters and hiring managers (only 7 percent). The positive candidate ratings jump upwards of 28 percent when they receive a phone versus the automated email rejection, a big difference that can go a long way.

EXAMPLES OF DELIGHT

Opportunities to delight your candidates are everywhere. Delighting a candidate (and an existing employee for that matter) can be quite simply thought of as *unexpected value at an unexpected time.* At Ph.Creative, we call it a *moment of magic.*

When was the last time you experienced unexpected value at an unexpected time? Recall that moment and ask yourself, *how did it make you feel?*

That *feeling* is *why* adding a Delight stage to your activation plan is so important. Not only does it make you stand out, but it's also memorable.

To get your brainstorming session started, we jotted down examples of external activation **Delight** that you can use as inspiration or simply build into your candidate experience.

STAGE OF CANDIDATE EXPERIENCE	MOMENT OF MAGIC (DELIGHT)
Career website application form	A small gift in return for giving feedback in a one-question pulse survey (or net promoter score [NPS] rating).
Candidate experience center	A warm and personal greeting on arrival using their name.
	Their favorite Starbucks drink waiting for them.
	A text welcoming them to campus and telling them where to go.
Rejection or "timing isn't right" letter	Detailed feedback on how to come back stronger or improve on specific areas of weakness.
	Access to resources to improve their résumé or interview skills (Career Arc's Candidate Care offering).
Offer letter	Having the letter signed by all the team you're joining.
	Videotext job offer recorded by hiring manager.

Hopefully, you see from the items listed above that it doesn't have to be an extravagance; it just needs to be obviously considerate, courteous, empathetic, and human.

To elevate the power of Delight significantly, imagine the biggest worries, doubts, biases, hopes, dreams, and fears that a candidate may have about joining your organization.

Now consider the power of matching your *Give and Get* with those feelings.

If you search for moments of magic using the lens of all the specifics you want people to experience when they meet your employer brand, you can tailor an experience that not only creates delight but one that also reinforces and adds credibility to your EVP by default.

For example, with Virgin, Ph.Creative worked to improve the candidate experience, which meant adhering to Virgin's brand guidelines: fun, generous, and supportive.

FUN:

Ph.Creative created Cut the Quack, an online portal where candidates can copy and paste their résumé only to find cliché or bland words replaced with ducks. When you shoot the ducks, it replaced them with better language.

It is a fun tool to use, but it's also generous and supportive because it helped to improve the first impression you make as a candidate.

GENEROUS:

Ph.Creative created a library full of career coaching resources designed to help you become a more employable candidate, whether you got a job at Virgin or not. Content ranged from best practice guides to how to make a good first impression. It covered how to approach answering typical interview questions to more advanced articles and videos talking about how to plan for your first hundred days on the job.

SUPPORTIVE:

Ph.Creative created a content series that changed as a candidate moved through the candidate experience. Content ranged from hiring managers describing the vibe of the office and what to expect when you come in, to an unexpected video message from Usain Bolt wishing you good luck the night before your interview.

Consider candidate journey mapping to identify exactly how and what a candidate feels, thinks, remembers, enjoys, and dislikes about your candidate experience. See Bryan's first book, *Getting Goosebumps*, for a complete guide.

CANDIDATE EXPERIENCE RESEARCH

There is a ton of external research available to help you strengthen your business case and to inform where you'll get the biggest ROI. Here are a few of our favorites:

- The Talent Board, North American Candidate Experience Research Report
- iCIMS, Candidate Experience Study
- *Bersin* by Deloitte, Talent Acquisition Factbook
- IBM Smarter Workforce Institute, The Far-Reaching Impact of Candidate Experience
- CareerBuilder, Candidate Experience from End to End
- CareerBuilder, Candidate Survey

- SmashFly, *Fortune* 500 Report: Recruitment Marketing Benchmarks
- Brandon Hall Group, The State of Recruitment Marketing
- CareerArc, Employer Branding Study

SUMMARY

"People will forget what you say, people will forget what you did, but people will never forget how you made them feel."

This quote is worth repeating as we summarize why the candidate experience is so important. And to prove it, the data shared in this chapter consistently shows that candidates who have had a negative candidate experience take their wallet and relationships somewhere else.

Since the industry has a lot to offer on this topic, we focused our advice on how to incorporate the *Give and Get* into your candidate experience. The key thing to remember is to incorporate moments of magic using the lens of all the things you want people to experience when they encounter your employer brand.

Most people focus on reducing friction or frustration from their candidate experience. In our opinion, real Delight occurs when you tailor an experience that reinforces your EVP by default. For example, if one of your EVPs talks about demanding work, part of your interview process may be a twenty-four-hour turnaround writing assignment. That's not easy or frustration-free, but it reinforces the demands of the job. By default, some will opt out of completing the assignment, and others will embrace it. That's how you repel the many, compel the few.

Up next: getting buy-in and developing a winning business case. Let's dive into how to navigate the politics at play and how to create a business case and approach that gets you to a world-class result.

MEASUREMENT, PEOPLE, AND POLITICS

HOW TO WIN FRIENDS AND INFLUENCE PEOPLE

"When dealing with people, remember you are not dealing with creatures of logic but creatures of emotion."

—DALE CARNEGIE

Getting buy-in and developing a winning business case separates the good employer brand leaders from the great employer brand leaders. In our opinion, it's a critical skill to hone and develop because most employer brand leaders find themselves in a newly created role that lacks the budget, headcount, and resources necessary to do their job. On top of that, the people they need to influence to get a budget are often new to employer brand and ask questions that can be hard to answer if you've never done this type of work before. After all:

- Most employer brand practitioners find their way into

employer brand from traditional marketing, communications, or recruiting roles.

- They learn on the job because you still can't earn a degree in employer brand while in school.
- They're typically junior in their career, meaning they are outmatched by the seniority of the people they need to influence.
- The people they must influence often don't understand how to build or activate an employer brand or why they should invest additional budget toward the work.
- It's hard to measure.
- Finally, often employer brand practitioners sit in HR but have the word *brand* in their title, which doesn't make fast friends with marketing, who may be annoyed or threatened by the perceived lack of departmental control.

The first six months of any new employer brand role involves heavy change management. Your goal is to build relationships across the organization—marketing, communications, HR, TA leadership, and recruiters—prove the value of your work, and secure the investment required to build your employer brand.

Yet at first glance, let's face it, you're the underdog.

So get ready to take notes, because this chapter provides the ammunition you need to fire to navigate the politics at play. Because when your business case stacks up, your work can quickly be a top priority in your organization.

BUILDING A BUSINESS CASE: START WITH *WHY*

Here's where you reinforce what you hope to achieve and how the employer brand can get you there.

- List three to five bullet points that are simple and clear.
- Numbers must be clear and impressive (improved quality of app, cost per hire/application, current stats about employer brand ROI).
- Show evidence for cultural improvement.
- Show evidence you will be behind the curve compared to competitors.
- Show evidence you will improve the existing priorities they have on their desk—if you look hard enough, you will find a people problem you can help with.

Another thing that helps influence a room of C-suite executives is to point out that the work being done is tactical if that's the case. We've seen many organizations suffering from post-and-pray attraction efforts, high RPO spend, and lack of metrics to support investments, to name a few. Since it's in a leader's DNA to be strategic, they'll likely be motivated by making a strategic investment that controls spend overtime.

So here's what you do.

Point out that in every business around the world, the cost of recruiting great talent is going up.

Therefore, if we continue to operate using the same tactics, it's going to get costlier and less efficient to fill our roles. There is a point of diminishing returns. We need to be strategic.

To a room of C-suite execs, it's reasonable to have them agree some change is necessary. The change you suggest is to make an up-front investment to develop talent attraction assets, much like a down payment for a house. Over time, your company will realize the gains of that up-front investment, and it starts paying you back. So rather than the expense of recruiting talent continuing to climb every year, it starts to level out.

To demonstrate the ROI, project the spend over the next three years. Show that the savings is more than the initial investment over time, like in the graphic below.

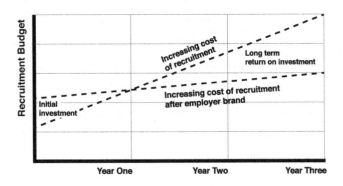

See the line going up? It represents the increasing cost of recruitment over time. We added a line to show what happens to that cost after activating an employer brand. While the cost will be more in year 1 since this is a new body of work that requires investment (see the red triangle), the thing to point out is how it levels out over time, rather than climbing. The section in green is the realized savings.

COST OF A ROLE STAYING VACANT

This simple formula may also help strengthen your case. It gives you the daily lost revenue of a role staying vacant at your organization. This formula gives you an average across your entire organization. It doesn't parse out revenue-generating roles such as sales versus nonrevenue-generating roles like administration, so it may be even higher if you crunch the numbers differently.

FORMULA:

Total company revenue (divided by) total number of employees (divided by 365) = Average revenue per employee per day.

Take the average revenue per employee per day (multiplied by) the total number of vacant roles = Total daily lost revenue.

The final figure is often staggering. If the average time to fill in the United States is forty days and you shave five days off that, the savings are noticeable.

Let's look at an actual business case. This next table shows you the exact points we created to demonstrate the value we were going to deliver at a health-care organization. The language and positioning under "What we must achieve" were aligned with the organization's priorities and goals.

The column on the right, "What we want," uses language to bring us all together as one. Knowing what we all want to accomplish is key to demonstrating how employer brand is the solution they've been waiting for but probably never knew existed.

WHY

What we must achieve before 2020	What we want
To have a highly visible and revered brand in the marketplace	Increase referrals
	Tap into passive market
To win the ever-increasing fight for the best talent in health care before it becomes unattainable	Reduce unqualified applicants
	Reduce cost and time to hire significantly
To find the right people to stay, who thrive and excel—contributing to our overall business goals	Reduce agency spend and voluntary new hire turnover

They had a goal to double their referral rate. It was the best source of hire and the least expensive, so it's a no-brainer to develop a referral program as part of this work.

The last two objectives hit on reducing the time and expense related to recruiting. I've worked for several TA leaders over the course of my career who made it their business to audit agency expenses and see just how much money was flying out of the window to RPOs. The number is often staggering. Say the figure was $15 million. If your TA team can take on some of the work that is being outsourced, at say $10 million, there is a good chance you'll get the additional resources, and the business also realizes significant cost savings.

Hopefully, sharing this example helps you see the ingredients needed to build a business case. After presenting your *why*, it should be apparent to everybody why we must do this. So then the natural question they should ask you next is *how*.

THE HOW

This is where you want to talk about the tangible outputs and other benefits you get such as:

- Higher quality applicants and hires
- Lower volume of applicants
- Advocacy/referrals
- Employee engagement
- Direct hire capability versus agency spend

How we can easily achieve both together	Conclusions we can agree on	The good news
Increase referrals to over 50 percent of all hires	We must reach the best talent, not just the talent looking for us.	We have a leadership team in touch with the business.
Increase engagement and retention levels	We must make our budget stretch further and work harder to gain momentum.	We have insatiable synergy, unity, and consistency throughout the organization—an incredible foundation to build on.
Stream people toward our brand including passive candidates	We must transition to strategic talent attraction and retention rather than tactical.	The journey has started; we built our employer brand in one hundred days.

At the end of the day when your numbers are clear and you show the evidence for cultural improvement, the buy-in happens.

GIVE THE POWER TO YOUR AUDIENCE

Because the age-old rules haven't changed—when you can't take the power, you must give the power. Ask yourself how can you give power to your audience?

Here are some ways we have given the power to our audience over the years to increase advocacy.

SHAREABLE UPDATES

Regular updates throughout the project engagement are important. At the onset, identify a list of key stakeholders as well as a list of research participants. Keeping them all well informed is key. And it's not just what you say; it's also how you say it.

Know your audience. If you need to influence a group of executives and you have an ally who knows them and is willing to help you (often, this will take the form of an HR leader), ask yourself how might you make them look good along the way? The easier you make it for people to help you, the more help you get.

For example, we always write communication updates for our stakeholders. This includes communications to socialize the project, invites to meetings, thank-you memos after the workshops, and so on. People are busy and appreciate having a polished tool kit ready to leverage.

This is also a great opportunity to think creatively and engage your audience. People don't read emails anymore, so leverage social, video, and text to engage your audience. Ph.Creative often gives their clients a two-minute movie trailer at the completion of the research phase. It serves as a preview of the key themes and insights and what's to come next. It's easily shareable internally and creates a sense of fun and excitement. If you know anyone who has worked with Ph.Creative to build their employer brand, send them a note and ask to see their movie trailer and chat about the excitement it generated for them.

IT'S NOT WHAT YOU SAY BUT HOW YOU SAY IT

Celebrate the people who help you and make them the star of the show. One way to do so is to let your employees launch the employer brand, rather than HR. Find those who participated in the build and draft a memo from them. Let them release it to their teams.

We did this a few years ago and it created high levels of advocacy and interest. After all, it was coming from someone they knew, trusted, and respected. Plus, it gave this group of stakeholders visibility and credit for their contributions. When the oohs and ahs started to come in, they heard them directly.

Write like a human, with the same care and attention you'd give to your external communications. Here's a memo example:

In April of this year, we gathered in Scottsdale, Arizona, for one specific reason—to talk about you. That day, we kicked off a journey to better understand you.

We asked, and you shared...your perspectives, opinions, passions, and voice—all toward articulating our talent brand, a brand that aptly captures and communicates exactly what it means to be part of this organization.

This week, we're ready to reveal the results.

It's our hope that this new launch will do you and your teams justice. We hope you will hear and see messages that you believe in, that ring true and accurately describe why and what our culture really feels like. One clear strength that resonated loud and clear throughout our research was our unrelenting collaborative and supportive spirit. We'd like to call on that spirit and ask you to help us share, celebrate, and enjoy this new employer brand to help us find more great people just like you.

But we'll get to that in due course. For now, just look, and feel free to share it with your team.

From,

[All stakeholders signature goes here]

MEASUREMENT

Employer brand management has become increasingly critical to business. Leading organizations around the world realize the benefits derived from the development of an EVP and a holistic employer brand strategy, including:

- Ability to attract higher quality and more qualified candidates at a lower cost.
- Reduction in overall recruitment costs and time to fill.
- Decrease in attrition rates.
- Increased employee engagement.

There are a variety of metrics you can use to gauge your team's performance and demonstrate brand effectiveness, which we list in this chapter. However, there are two in particular that we want you to focus on:

1. Unwanted applicants
2. Regrettable loss

UNWANTED APPLICANTS (KEY ATTRACTION METRIC)

After applying the *Give and Get* philosophy, start to watch your unwanted applicants, a term we learned from Andrew Gadomski, a workforce and HR data scientist and analyst and managing director of Aspen Analytics.

Unwanted applicants are the ones who are dismissed at various stages and their origination.

"In larger scale businesses, especially those that collect more than thirty applicants per job, it's critical to reduce the number of nos a business executes. A smart employer brand can reduce incoming applicants and escalate the brand impact at the same time."

—ANDREW GADOMSKI

By tracking this key metric, you start to see the effectiveness of your *Give and Get* proposition at work. If you can evidence a reduction of unwanted applications, you can prove that more potential ill-fitting candidates are self-selecting out.

This should also correlate to your caliber of hire. We want to see your caliber of hire go up without the extra strain on your recruitment efforts to sift through a significantly increased volume of applicants to find them.

REGRETTABLE LOSS (KEY RETENTION METRIC)

Every organization talks about retention, and usually it's from a perspective that when people leave, that's a bad thing, and when people stay, that's a good thing. So the metric of retention will be discussed in terms of a requirement to retain more people.

In our experience, when you talk to a leader in any healthy organization, this is not the case. Usually, there are people you would actually like to see leave because they're merely surviving, rather than thriving. And then there's the top performers you would never want to do without.

Imagine a company that had one thousand employees and your retention rate was 99 percent. Only ten people left each year. Most organizations would think that was incredible. But what if those ten people were your top performers and rising stars? Worse yet, what if they had valuable intellectual property that would be very hard to replace? If you knew that ten of your best people were leaving to join your biggest talent competitors each year, what would you do? Your regrettable loss is at 100 percent, and now you have a big problem on your hands. Retaining this level of top talent is a business imperative.

Now imagine the same company with a retention rate of just 75 percent. Two hundred and fifty people were leaving each year, and it was costing the business a significant amount to replace them. The conventional and typical report might suggest you have a terrible employee engagement and retention problem on your hands. However, what if out of those two hundred and fifty people, your hiring managers would not rehire any of them. If you have no regrettable loss (0 percent), you have a huge opportunity to drive positive change. Yes, it comes at a price and it might cause disruption; however, if you're now attracting more of the right candidates, your organization is about to level up with a very significant increase in caliber of hire. This quality of hire is something that should be measured and used for future regrettable loss data.

After applying the *Give and Get* philosophy, watch your regrettable loss numbers change. As discussed previously, the first big opportunity to capitalize on with your new employer brand and EVP is to re-recruit the talent you already have. This requires a strong and ongoing internal activation strategy. Use your new EVP to remind your rising stars and top talent why they're at your organization, and show them how much they are appreciated.

"More CEOs and their board of directors are starting to rank

talent issues as highly as financial issues in the board room. Regrettable loss is a key metric to determine an organization's health. Companies can and should take action to make an incredible difference."

—CHER MURPHY, CHIEF PEOPLE OFFICER, PH.CREATIVE

FINDING YOUR DIALS

Agree on what success looks like at the start of the engagement so you know what to measure along the way. The tools available include paid media metrics, CRM/ATS data, surveys, NPS, career site conversion and traffic metrics, quality of app/hire, and time and cost to fill, to name a few. No matter which metrics you choose to follow, make sure unwanted applicants are one of them.

While there are a variety of metrics to consider, it's important to align your goals with business objectives. For example, your company may want to reduce its reliance on agency or RPO spend. Or they may have a focus on reducing time to fill or completing hiring targets for a hard-to-fill job category. Perhaps you are opening a new office in a location where no one knows you.

Ask yourself, can your work help fill those jobs on time? We think so. The key is to pick two to three areas you'll focus on and pick a measurement to guide your work with a lens on improvement. If a baseline metric doesn't exist, year 1 may be setting a baseline and working to improve upon it over time.

METRICS THAT MATTER

Not every leadership is driven by costs. It's important to find the numbers and indicators that resonate and improve the performance of existing business priorities.

Importantly, no organization benefits from measuring a new set of metrics in a vacuum, especially if they don't understand the value of them. Therefore, it's essential that whatever new metrics you choose to track, you can also demonstrate how those new numbers impact numbers that the company already values.

For example, if you start to track your Glassdoor and Comparably ratings, your candidate experience NPS, and an employee happiness NPS, as those numbers start to go up, it would be infinitely more valuable if you can correlate this improvement with increased caliber of talent hired, a reduction in attrition, or an increase in company-wide employee referrals.

Ideally, you want to be able to prove a derivative of improvement to the performance of existing goals in your organization. What's more, if these existing goals are a priority of your senior leadership, the value of your work will be recognized, understood, and appreciated a whole lot more.

This approach is infinitely easier and more effective than downloading a generic employer brand dashboard off the internet and circulating a new set of numbers the organization doesn't understand or care about.

Our advice is to use those dashboards and recommendations in this book as inspiration for what you should be measuring. Some generic and commonly noted metrics to consider can be found below. You can use this as a starting point to get a sense of priority within your stakeholder group, then add any specific metrics that your company cares about. Use the priority rating to narrow down your measurement and tracking to a minimum number of critical monthly metrics that are easy to gather.

METRIC	CURRENT	TARGET	PRIORITY LEVEL
Engagement and sentiment metrics			
Glassdoor rating	3.6	4.5	High
Comparably rating	65/100	80/100	High
Candidate NPS	−21	+50	Average
Recruiter NPS	+12	+25	Low
Hiring manager NPS	+12	+25	Low
Employee NPS	+12	+55	High
Brand awareness	60%	80%	High
Career website behavior metrics			
Bounce rate	60%	10%	High
Time on site	45 seconds	2 minutes	Average
Depth of visit	2 pages	6 pages	Average
Site traffic volume	33,000/month	75,000/month	High
Returning visitor ratio	2:1	1:1	Average
Number of top ten SEO keyword rankings	12	100	High
Application conversion rate	12%	50%	High
Social media metrics			
Engagement rate	12%	40%	Average
Brand sentiment score	20% positive	60% positive	High
LinkedIn Following	12,000	24,000	Low
Facebook following	5,000	50,000	Low
Instagram following	12,000	100,000	High
Twitter following	30,000	50,000	Average
YouTube following	900	25,000	Average
Passive candidate applications	8%	33%	High

METRIC	CURRENT	TARGET	PRIORITY LEVEL
Recruiting metrics			
Offer to acceptance rate	90%	100%	High
Retention rate	85%	95%	Average
Regrettable loss rate	15%	0%	High
Valuable applicant rate	60%	90%	High
Quality of hire			
Average cost of application	$3.50	$1.50	High
Average cost of hire	$1,200	$900	High
Average time to hire	9 weeks	6 weeks	High
Talent flow in (from known key talent competitor)	53 people from company X	120 people from company X	High
Talent flow out (from known key talent competitor)	12 people from company X	0 people from company X	
Employee referral rate	10%	40%	High
Earned media value of employee advocacy	$1,000,000	$2,000,000	Average
Source of hire	Indeed	Google and career website	High

LEVERAGING YOUR RESULTS

Now that you are measuring your work, find a way to socialize the numbers with key stakeholders. After all, the key to growing your value internally is closely attached to your ability to prove the impact you are having.

We like setting up a monthly scorecard that you can share with your manager that they can easily forward on to their leadership. Your boss wants to report on progress; the easier you make it to absorb and understand, the more likely they hit the forward button on your monthly report. Keep in mind, this is also the time to call out what isn't working and why, attached with a request for budget to solve the issue.

We see too many employer brand leaders showing how much they do with a zero-dollar budget. Unfortunately, the more you highlight what you do for zero dollars, the more likely you are to keep your budget at a standstill. If adding budget will help you solve something quicker or make a bigger impact, ask for it. Then measure it and show ROI. You can start small using this approach; over time, your credibility will increase, and your asks get easier.

SUMMARY

In conclusion, getting buy-in and developing a winning business case separates the good employer brand leaders from the great employer brand leaders. It's a critical skill to hone and develop because it's the key to advancing your career and growing your value internally.

- Start with *why*, reinforce what you hope to achieve and how the employer brand can get you there.
- Show them *how*, talk about the tangible outputs.
- When you can't take the power, give the power to your audience. Always think about how you can make it easy for someone to support your work.
- Set up measurements and share your progress.
- Track unwanted applicants and regrettable loss.

As we near the end of the book, the last two chapters cover the way we define key employer brand terms, such as pillars, EVP, brand essence, and so on. We share examples to better illustrate what good, great, and world class looks like for each area so you can see them in practice. We also cover how long each can stay relevant and when to refresh.

If you are an experienced professional, you may want to skip the next chapter and jump straight into "Resources, Reading, and Final Thoughts."

EMPLOYER BRAND
AND EVP DEFINED

The job of an employer brand practitioner is to brand and market the employment experience of a given company. First, you define a common understanding of the universal experience of working at an organization, and then you create communication campaigns to tell everyone about it.

Our approach to EVP is to identify the Give and the Get to articulate not only the benefits, strengths, and opportunities someone receives from working at your organization but also the demands, expectations, and realities of what it takes to really thrive.

By defining the Give and the Get of employee experience, employees clearly know what is expected of them and what they can expect of you as an employer. It works to attract and retain talent who is a good culture match or culture add, while equally repelling those who are not.

Our goal is to create an employer brand platform that

reflects an employer's organizational performance objectives and drives attraction, engagement, and retention of talent who will thrive at our organization.

OUR DEFINITIONS

- **Employer Brand:** How people describe what it's like to work at your organization.
- **Employer Brand Essence:** An overarching positioning statement that serves as an accurate depiction of the intent and reality of the employee experience. It is a compelling, single idea that provides focus for creative expression and alignment to the corporate brand and the values at the core of the organization, too.
- **Employer Brand Story:** A long-form version of your employer brand essence in story format. This story is designed to expand on the idea framed by the employer brand essence and to bring more clarity and insight into what it means to work at your organization. It is a good practice to have two versions of the employer brand story nuanced for both the internal and external talent audiences.
- **Employer Brand Pillar:** An overarching, universal common theme of the employee experience. An employer brand can have any number of pillars supporting the main employer brand essence.
- **EVP/AVP:** Clear propositions designed to provide insight and clarity around what your talent must be

willing to *give* your organization in return for what they can *get* from your organization. These propositions are designed to crystallize what kind of people thrive at your organization and why they should care.

- **Persona:** An archetypical representation of one segment of your talent audience. Persona provides points of emphasis for functional and/or geographic talent segments that help translate and tailor the EVP in a meaningful way to communicate more effectively with each different target audience you have. Segmenting your talent audience into different personas provides the opportunity to understand and cater to which of the different brand strengths, benefits, opportunities, and expectations to dial up or down depending on their motivators and drivers, preferences and priorities.

A FEW EXAMPLES
THE BRAND ESSENCE

Usually an aspirational headline, the brand essence exists to inspire and engage an audience by piquing their interest and drawing them in closer toward the company. Quite often, the brand essence will articulate intention and tap into the purpose of the organization. An effective brand essence will resonate with people's values and align with lifestyle, ideals, and ambition.

A lot of organizations present the essence as one main publicly facing EVP. This could well be the reason that even many HR professionals confuse the difference between the employer brand essence and an EVP. Can you see how this can be a dangerous and even misleading prospect if that same brand essence *is* your EVP?

One message designed to resonate with the entire populous of a talent audience needs to be quite the charming statement, right? It can be done, but it's a lot to ask. If it's too aspirational, it runs the risk of being too lofty and generic. Too specific and wordy, it risks becoming complicated, or awkward, or just not very memorable.

However, an employer brand essence, just like a regular brand, should be able to stand the test of time. An EVP is like your shop window. It needs to stay fresh and remain relevant to the talent market, which means the EVP can change more frequently. Unless you have only one proposition that can paint an accurate description of your employee experience and resonate with your entire talent audience, the chances are, your organization requires more than one EVP to help you illustrate the full picture of your employee experience.

EMPLOYER BRAND ESSENCE EXAMPLES:

"Be you with us" by Cisco. It's timeless, simple, and very clear that they're all about embracing people for who they are

in a place where it's OK to be yourself. Very smart. The EVP messaging beneath can change to flex and evolve as the audience's interpretation, preferences, and priorities change without the need to update the essence.

"Bring everything you are, become everything you want" by SAP. This is a similar variation of Cisco's employer brand essence. It's not short and sharp, but it has an element of value exchange and forward-facing inspiration that's more about you than them, which is commendable. It also suggests inclusivity, career progression, support, and achievement.

"Transform your everyday" by Salesforce. This is an upbeat call to action that's incredibly simple yet inspirational, playing on the fact that we all go to work every day, so why can't we enjoy it? It's positive, suggestive, and inviting.

EMPLOYER BRAND PILLARS

Employer brand pillars show what a company deems to be most important or prominent in their culture in terms of strengths to be found, appreciated, and leveraged. The subsequent messaging often provides social proof because quite often you see and read the words of existing employees, which is appreciated, and it does inspire more confidence than faceless corporate language.

STRONG EMPLOYER BRAND PILLAR EXAMPLES:

Once again, Salesforce is a good example of the effective use of traditional EVP pillars supporting an employer brand essence. In fact, Salesforce does a great job of explicitly presenting their pillars in a way that makes the proposition very attractive and widely appealing.

"Meaningful work" speaks to purpose.

"Good people" suggests the people are, well, good! They talk about their values, behaviors, and trusted relationships, which makes the brand seem inclusive and human.

"Unparalleled rewards" addresses the benefit of working at a high-performing organization filled with driven and passionate smart people who achieve outstanding results.

HOW LONG CAN AN EVP AND EMPLOYER BRAND STAY RELEVANT?

While your employer brand can stay constant for three to five years, the EVP must be sense checked annually. This is because as the needs, wants, and desires of the market shift, your EVP should evolve to stay relevant to the market.

If an employer brand reflects who you truly are, the EVP is a current snapshot of current reality and why people should care about who you are. The why can change, should change, as the wants, needs, desires, and marketplace changes and evolves over time.

The research you gather has a half-life that will vary in length depending on the pace of your market. However, if it takes you twelve months to realize the research and insights you've gathered, they're probably already somewhat out of date. To be relevant, the time it takes you to conduct your research on brand activation must be less than six months. The employer brand may remain the same for four or five years, but the EVP should be refreshed and sense checked annually.

WHAT DOES A WORLD-CLASS EMPLOYER BRAND LOOK LIKE?

In the last decade, we've seen a variety of approaches to employer brand. In our experience, there are elements that create a clear separation between what good, great, and world class looks like.

Entry-level employer brand

Usually, a defined employer brand has a memorable tagline, underpinned by traditional brand pillars. These pillars help to define the makeup of the brand and group together the essential ingredients that make an organization unique. These pillars are typically underpinned and cross-checked with corporate values.

Basic Give and Get employer brand

A basic *Give and Get* employer brand is authentic and believable enough for employees to agree that it's a fair representation of the best version of your organization on any given day. A great employer brand will be transparent enough to also acknowledge the more aspirational aspects but provide a genuine rationale and a narrative around the reality of today and the reality of tomorrow.

World-class Give and Get employer brand

A world-class *Give and Get* employer brand also uses the adversity or gaps found within the employee experience to elevate the purpose, reality, and aspiration of your employee experience in line with your company vision. It conveys a sense of who belongs, the impact that can be made, and why it should be so purposeful and meaningful to everyone in the organization.

WHAT DOES A WORLD-CLASS EVP LOOK LIKE?

Entry-level EVP

An EVP is the intentional positioning and marketing of your employer brand, aimed at putting the employer brand in the best, most relevant light for your audience—namely, employees and candidates.

Basic Give and Get EVP

A basic *Give and Get* EVP will resonate with people who align with your core values and beliefs but also be strong enough to repel those who are not suited to your organization. It's not about appealing to everyone; it's about appealing to everyone who will thrive and significantly contribute toward the mission within your organization.

An effective EVP requires tailoring for each specific lens of your audience segment, to speak to them in their language, and context the employer brand in the most relevant and significant light to them as possible.

World-class Give and Get EVP

A world-class EVP not only resonates effectively with the right type of people for your organization, but it also clearly lays out the Give and the Get for people so they can see what's expected of them to move the business forward and what they can expect to benefit from in return.

This means a world-class EVP needs to elicit an emotional connection with an audience that either pulls a person closer toward your brand or pushes them further away with great effectiveness based on the ability to answer the underlying questions surrounding impact, purpose, and belonging.

To do this, we must truly understand what motivates, drives, and inspires the people we're looking for on two basic levels that address and satisfy the whole person, not just the professional side of an employee, all sides of a human being, both rationally and emotionally. And once we understand this from the audience's perspective, we must dig deeper and discover why, how, and specifically what contributes toward these factors.

By putting the EVP in the context of an employee's inward (emotional) and outward (rational) motivation, people can choose or instinctively get a sense of whether they want to be part of your organization, whether they can add value, and whether they could feel valued as part of your team.

By taking this basic, human approach, we can be both prescriptive and specific, as well as be diverse and inclusive.

A world-class EVP is updated frequently, in line with the rate of change of your business and your audience (employees and candidates) wants, needs, demands, and desires. An EVP that is a true reflection of last year's business will help you attract and keep the talent fit for an environment you need to complete last year's goals. If the goals and the competitive landscape are the same, good. If the goals and competitive landscape have changed, you must be willing to adapt and update with it or risk being less relevant, less competitive, and less effective.

SUMMARY

We want you to aspire to be world class in each of the key areas described in this chapter because they directly impact your ability to repel the many and compel the few.

If you are starting out as the first employer brand practitioner in your organization, you have the gold standard to apply. If you are joining a team that already has elements of employer brand in place, you can use this to audit the strength of your employer brand and recommend ways to fill the gaps that may be present.

In the final chapter, we offer up a wealth of resources, additional reading, and ways to connect with a tribe of employer brand practitioners whom we are honored to work alongside.

RESOURCES, READING, AND FINAL THOUGHTS

"Be so good they can't ignore you."

—STEVE MARTIN

In 2019, we did a phenomenal job convincing the employers the value of employer brand, demonstrated by the thousands of new employer brand roles opened around the world at companies big and small.

We're starting to see momentum pick up because the *perceived* value of attracting the right talent into an organization is now aligning with the *reality* of how important it is to grow and scale any business successfully. This means that the role TA and employer brand professionals play has never been more aligned to the CEO's strategic plans (and can very well be the difference between hitting the goals or not).

Many of these newly donned employer professionals will spend their first year bottling the magic of their organization, finding what makes their company different, and defining what makes them special. It will be thrilling, and often lonely, as many of you are the only person in your company doing this work.

If you remember only one thing from this chapter, what we would like it to be is this: you have a tremendous community of employer brand professionals, conferences, networks, and peers waiting to collaborate with you. A few of our favorites are listed here.

And just in case you feel alone, battling the politics at play in your organization, read this first. I (Charlotte) have lived this experience six times over now, and one thing is the same each time—six months of heavy change management followed by HR versus marketing politics, which is why I want to share this with you.

WHAT IT FEELS LIKE TO WORK IN EMPLOYER BRAND TODAY:
DAVID VERSUS GOLIATH

Three thousand years ago, two armies found themselves in a deadlock. To avoid the heavy bloodshed of open battle, each side chose one warrior to represent them in a duel.

The Philistines sent their greatest warrior, a giant named Goliath. He was 6 feet 9 inches. To protect himself against blows to the body, he wore an elaborate tunic made up of hundreds of overlapping bronze fishlike scales. It covered his arms and reached to his knees and weighed more than one hundred pounds. He had bronze plates protecting his legs and feet. He had three separate weapons, all optimized for close combat.

On the opposing side, only one person volunteered to go up against the giant. They tried to talk David, a young shepherd, out of going, saying he was outmatched. Yet, he was adamant. He had faced more ferocious opponents than this. When the lion or the bear came to carry off a sheep from the herd, he would go after the predator and strike it down and rescue the prey.

When they tried to dress David in armor, he refused. "I cannot walk in these," he said, "for I am unused to it." Instead, he reaches down and picks up five smooth stones and puts them in his shoulder bag. Then he descends into the valley, carrying his shepherd's staff.

Goliath looks at the boy coming toward him, insulted. He was expecting to do battle with a seasoned warrior. What he didn't know was that David had no intention of following the conventional battle strategy.

During his approach, David quickly put one of his stones into the leather pouch of a sling and fires at Goliath's exposed forehead. Goliath falls. David runs toward him, seizes his sword, and cuts off the giant's head.

As employer brand leaders, we also face giants—the numerous obstacles that stand between us and the investment we need to do our jobs. And like David, at first glance, we are outmatched by the seniority of those we must influence and certainly by lack of budget, head count, and resources that accompany our roles.

WHY IT'S HARD TO NAVIGATE

Most of us found our way into employer brand from traditional marketing or recruiting roles. You still can't study employer branding in school, and most of us are junior in our career when we take our first employer branding roles. It doesn't take long, however, to discover that the people we must influence for budget, head count, and buy-in don't often understand the value of employer brand simply because it's so new.

And then there is this one little word in our title that makes the people we need to partner most with uneasy—*brand.* If your title says some form of "employer brand" and you report into HR, you know what I am talking about.

THE OPPORTUNITY

So yes, it can be hard at first, but if you remember only one thing from this book, I'd like it to be this: employer brand is an essential ingredient to any business looking to scale, grow, and achieve significant accomplishment. Time and time again, I've seen the impact a strong employer brand can make on an organization. Yet, for that magic to occur, you must first learn how to navigate the politics at play within your organization.

What do you think would have happened if David followed conventional thinking and fought Goliath on his terms? He would have been absolutely pulverized! David knew Goliath's perceived strengths were weaknesses. That heavy armor made him slow, his size and health condition made it so he couldn't see very well. So rather than waiting for an up-close and personal confrontation, David quickly drew a rock from his bag and fired from the distance, substituting speed and surprise for physical strength.

After more than fifteen years of developing, launching, and driving employer brand and EVPs around the world, I am sharing a few tips to help you build and deploy your next employer brand in a simple, yet powerful, way. As a result, it is my hope that you apply the bits that resonate with you to define the employee experience of your organization in a way that inspires, moves, and resonates with the audiences you need to reach.

If we knew then what we know now...

Perhaps the biggest surprise each time I take a new employer brand role is just how similar the challenges are within different organizations. Here are a few key learnings:

Move with pace and flexibility. Because just like David, it's our number one advantage. David wasn't bogged down wearing a bronze helmet, body armor, carrying a javelin, a spear, or a sword as Goliath did. He wore simple shepherd's clothing and carried a slingshot. His power came when he substituted speed and surprise for physical strength.

I developed an employer brand in just one hundred days. Conventional thinking is twelve to eighteen months, yet moving at that pace gave us more advocacy, more relevancy, and secured the investment we needed to do the work. Speed was our advantage.

Use the tools you have, not the tools you want. David could have been jealous of the shield, the armor, the sword, or the strength Goliath possessed. That's just like being jealous of marketing's budget, head count, resources, and control. Just remember you can't buy a shiny strapline. The only way to uncover the truth within your organization is to really listen. Do the research to get the key insights.

You have an opportunity to use real human emotion and

story to win the hearts and minds of your candidates and coworkers. The stories that people care about live with us. We find them. We tell them.

Ensure continuity of the person listening at the front and thinking at the end. Because some things just don't translate in a creative brief. Most agencies that you'll hire to support you are not structured to have the same team members work on each step of your engagement. Ensuring continuity of the same person moving from research to strategy to creative is critical. It's where the magic happens.

Give the power to your audience. Because the age-old rules haven't changed (when you can't take the power, you must give the power). Ask yourself, how can you give power to your audience?

Be brave. Because sometimes you've got to be brave to challenge convention. I hope as an industry, we can collectively continue to be brave and challenge convention but, more importantly, continue to share our successes and our failures so we all move forward together.

Get marketing on board. Because like many others before me, I have suffered the slings and arrows from working against marketing/brand teams. Design an approach that will help you win friends and influence people. After all, when it's a mutual value exchange, everyone is happy.

Communities, events, and tools. The employer brand community is the most welcoming, supportive, and fun community we have ever been a part of. Since we are all learning together as we go, there is little pride in ownership or idea. If something works, we share our learnings across the community. We willingly give our templates, resources, and recommendations with ease.

We also all talk, so if we have a poor experience with your product or service, there is a very good chance our words of caution will spread.

Facebook. Facebook has two active community groups: the Employer Brand Forum and the Talent Brand Alliance. We find the former to skew to the more experienced practitioners, whereas the latter skews to a greener audience.

ESSENTIAL READING AND INSPIRATION

PODCASTS

ChatTalent Podcast
CXR Podcast
DriveThru HR
Employee Cycle Podcast
HBR/IdeaCast
HR Happy Hour
HR Leaders
HR Power Hour
HR Studio Podcast
HR Works
HRExaminer
Illuminate HR Podcast
Impact Makers
Inevitable: The Future of Work
Let's Fix Work
Nine to Thrive
Real Job Talk
Recruiting Animal Recruiting
Brainfood Recruiting Daily
Recruiting Future Podcast
Recruitment on the Go
RecTech Podcast
Ruch Riffs
Science 4 Hire
Secrets of Staffing Success
Short, Tall & Ginger
Stanton Chase on Executive
Search and Leadership
Strong Suit
Talent Talk Radio
Talented
Talk Talent to Me Podcast
TaPod
TechRecruit Podcast
The #SocialRecruiting Show
The Chad & Cheese Podcast
The Emotionally Intelligent
Recruiter
The Employer Branding Podcast
The HR Social Hour

EVENTS

Australasian Talent
Conference
CareerXroads
ERE Recruiting Conference
Galvanize (Fairygodboss)
HCI Strategic Talent
Acquisition Summit
Hacking HR
Hiring Success
HR Unleash
IAMPHENOM
Indeed Interactive
Jobvite Recruiter Nation Live
LinkedIn Talent Connect
www.Ph-Creative.com/events
RallyFwdTM Virtual Conference
RecFest
RecruitCon
SHRM Annual Conference &
Exposition
SHRM Talent Conference
SourceCon
Talent Acquisition Week
Talent Brand Summit
TalentNet Live
Top Talent Summit Calgary
Top Talent Summit Toronto
World Employer Branding Day

TOOLS AND TECH

Altru
Beamery
CareerArc
Canva
Grammarly
HR.com
JobPageGrader.com
Humu
Linkedin Elevate
Paradox (Olivia)
Path Motion
Social Talent

ONLINE READING

www.chieflearningofficer.com
www.ere.net
www.giveandget.net
hbr.org
www.hrdigitaltrends.com
www.hrdive.com
hrexecutive.com
hr-gazette.com
www.hr.com
www.hrps.org
www.hrreporter.com
www.ph-creative.com/blog
www.recruiter.com
recruitingdaily.com
blog.shrm.org
www.sourcecon.com
theundercoverrecruiter.com
www.tlnt.com
www.workitdaily.com
workology.com

CREATIVE THINKING AND WORKING	CULTURE, LEADERSHIP, AND STRATEGY	PSYCHOLOGY AND BEHAVIORAL SCIENCE
Creativity Inc	The Advantage	The Laws of Human Nature
The War of Art	The Fearless Organization	Nudge
Rebel Ideas	The Barcelona Way	12 Rules for Life
The Creativity Curve	The 5 Temptations of a CEO	Atomic Habits
Messy	Start with Why	The Awakened Ape
Thinking Fast and Slow	Gung Ho! & Raving Fans	Propaganda
The Inspiration Code	The Culture Code	The Chimp Paradox
Deep Work	Dare to Lead	Mindset
Originals	Radical Candor	Never Split the Difference
Purple Cow	Exponential Organizations	How to Win Friends & Influence People
Contagious	Multipliers	
Love Marks	Getting Goosebumps	Black Box Thinking
Meaningful	Illuminate	Bounce
X: The Experience When Business Meets Design	Good to Great	Invisible Influence
Peak		

FINAL THOUGHTS

"Your work is going to fill a large part of your life, and the only way to be truly satisfied is to do what you believe is great work. And the only way to do great work is to love what you do."

—STEVE JOBS

We believe the *Give and Get* approach to employer brand and EVP is a tougher road to walk when it comes to defining and communicating who you are as an organization compared to a more traditional approach. We also recognize the difficulty to resist the urge to brag about the strengths, benefits, and opportunities of your brand, especially when you're incredibly proud of where you work.

However, we owe it to our existing people and those considering joining us to tell the whole truth about what can be expected as well as what's possible. It's the only way to bring real happiness to people and, in turn, sustainable success to our organizations.

If people don't hear the truth from you, they'll hear it somewhere else, or worse, they'll experience it after making a potentially wrong decision to join you in the first place.

If our employer brand and EVP does not have the ability to quickly put someone to a meaningful decision about our organization, we've not delivered well enough on our proposition.

Personal impact, purpose, belonging, and the adversity involved in finding fulfillment for each within your organization must be addressed up front. Everything else is window dressing.

We want you to leave this book inspired and committed to making a significant contribution to the quality of hundreds, thousands, or even millions of people's lives by getting this right. By defining your *Give and Get*, you have the power to help your organization find people who will thrive, not just survive.

And as Bryan always says, "People are the only true competitor advantage left in business today." Make the most of it. Your time is now.

ABOUT THE AUTHORS

BRYAN

Bryan Adams is CEO and founder of Ph.Creative, an internationally acclaimed employer-branding agency with offices and clients across the world. Founded in 2004, Bryan started his journey of entrepreneurship in branding and digital design before narrowing the focus toward employer branding and talent attraction in 2008 with the help of an amazing team.

The combination of his unusual route into the industry and surrounding himself with incredibly talented, creative, and curious people have inspired Bryan to develop and evolve a unique employer brand framework based on a passion for human behavior and the power of storytelling.

His unconventional approach has attracted some of the world's largest brands and smartest minds toward his agency such as Apple, Virgin, and Continental, and so the learning and evolving relentlessly continues.

Ph.Creative is renowned for delivering distinctive, creative, and memorable employer brand and candidate experience because of the philosophy and methodology found within this book, plus the hard work and collaboration of his seventy-plus-person team.

Bryan has interviewed more than fifty of the world's greatest storytellers including Seth Godin, Gary Vaynerchuk, and Robert McKee to strengthen knowledge and to fuel a passion for what it means to effectively move people with language.

He is a recognized social media influencer and creative strategist, a writer for Inc.com, and the coauthor of the best-selling book *Getting Goosebumps*, a pragmatic guide to content marketing for talent attraction.

Bryan is an engaging public speaker. His view of the world is often described as insightful, entertaining, thought-provoking, and unconventional.

CHARLOTTE

Named the 2019 Employer Brand Leader of the Year, Charlotte has a track record of successfully building and launching five different *Fortune* 500 employer brands. Her work inspires and enables marketing, communication, and HR professionals to attract the talent their businesses need to grow and scale.

As an award-winning employer brand influencer and speaker, she offers more than fifteen years of experience in driving large-scale global employer brand strategy and development in highly complex organizations, building robust cross-functional teams and alliances while cutting the time and expense it typically takes to do this work in half.

She has successfully led companies, departments, and highly complex global programs and initiatives. She contributed to significant talent attraction efforts to find a higher caliber of talent while also engaging and retaining top performers through the power of employer branding.

She is a highly sought-after international speaker and prolific member of the employer brand community.

HOW THIS BOOK CAME ABOUT

We (Charlotte and Bryan) met in early 2017. I (Charlotte) had just joined Magellan Health as vice president of Digital/Social Media and Employer Brand where I cut the time and cost the industry says it typically takes to develop an employer brand in half, working and thinking alongside the talented team at Ph.Creative.

This was important because like all new roles in the employer brand, I faced a seemingly insurmountable challenge to get the budget, buy-in, and the support I needed to do the work I was hired to accomplish.

Having done this exercise a few times before, I wanted to approach the work at Magellan differently. In the end, it took less than thirty minutes, an ask for a small budget, combined with the promise of realizing a significant return on that investment in the same financial year.

The green light was granted on the spot.

I secured the $100,000 investment needed to build Magellan's employer brand because my argument was compelling, different, brave, and ambitious. I took the role at Magellan because I was looking for a challenge and knew there had to be a better way to approach building an employer brand. This was the moment I knew I had made the right decision.

PAVING A NEW WAY

The initial employer brands I spearheaded took twelve to eighteen months to develop and varied in cost between $300,000 to $1,000,000 to complete. Beyond the time and cost associated, I realized that much of my later work resulted in higher application volumes that ended up drowning my team's funnels with unqualified applicants.

Yet, at the time, application volume was a measure of

success. When I was asked to share the Thermo Fisher Scientific case study for the first time at SmashFly's conference *Transform*, I remember hearing a lot of praise for the work followed by "*Charlotte, I just don't have the resources that you have. How can I achieve similar results without the budget or head count that you have?*"

This trend continued everywhere I spoke over the next twelve months. Growing tired of this line of thinking, I sought out a new opportunity at a *Fortune* 500 company that had resource constraints. I wanted to prove that it was possible to achieve world-class results without the resources I had had previously.

Joining Magellan gave me an opportunity to innovate. In the absence of a budget, I had creativity, autonomy, and foresight at my disposal. I sought out to find a new agency partner who wouldn't break the bank, who would think differently, and who had a strong creative department that would help us stand apart from everything else on the market.

A peer referred me to Ph.Creative, and the rest is history. Together, Bryan and I built Magellan's employer brand in one hundred days for $100,000, and the advantages went far beyond time and cost savings.

The activation surpassed the immediate targets we set

and quickly went on to become the first of its kind to be adopted as the full-fledged, overarching global brand of a *Fortune* 500 company, winning multiple awards along the way.

Looking back, much of the success can be attributed to the simple notion, two minds are better than one. Combining the insights of an experienced practitioner with the philosophy and approach of a progressive agency was powerful.

WHO THIS BOOK IS FOR

This book is for professionals with responsibility for people within an organization. That starts right at the top with CEOs and C-suite business leaders, through to employer brand leaders and everyone touching employee and candidate experience.

For CEOs, we hope you buy into the principles, get further insight into what to listen out for, what to empower, and what to authorize with priority and principle.

For practiced employer brand professionals, we hope to encourage you to embrace our philosophy and widen your approach to include a prominent *Give and Get* value exchange. We hope you feedback to us, too; we'd love to hear your thoughts and new experiences.

For those just starting out in employer brand, most of all we want to inspire you to think differently, work smart, keep learning, and feel compelled to help your organization clearly articulate the truth about their employee experience to great effect.

LEARN FROM THE AUTHORS

Bryan and Charlotte offer in-person workshops and can speak at your next event. Visit www.giveandget.net to learn more.

ACKNOWLEDGMENTS

We would like to thank the following people for making this book possible:

Charles Moyle, Craig Thomas, Kimberly Price, Sophia Whelan-Winsauer, Molly Perlich, Courtney Browne, Tammy Bustin Du-Pont, Kristine Balicoco, Boguslav Yanishen, Brian Sowards, David Hazelhurst, Samantha Hindley, Helen Adams, Michael Hazlehurst, Samantha Fawson, Tracey West, Natalie Price, Georgia Graham, Rory Palmer Rowe, Stefan Shaw, Neil Dutton, Andrew Grant, Georgina Ingham Clark, Robyn Campbell, Hollie Owens, James Millington, Julie Randall, Terry Adams, Alex Cowley, Tam Silah, Sian Holmes, Natalie Philip, John McNally, Jamie Cooper, Anna Newman, Clare Deacon, Jade Palmer Rowe, Joseph Rowen, Naoise McNabb, Paola Paulucci, James Taylor, Heather Duvall, Luke Power, Alison Wheeler, Anthony Whitelaw, Daniel Booth, Michelle Riches, Robert Watts, Elizabeth McCarthy, Paul Mason, Hannah Kirby, James Hendy, Glynn Powell, Jacqueline Steele, Amy Forrester, Michael Biggs, Nick Moss, Candice Chavalier, Christopher Davies, Cher

Murphy, Gerry Crispin, Lars Schmidt, Miki Johnson, Tim Sackett, Michael Smith, Ed Nathanson, Bari Polay, Craig Fisher, John Vlastelica, Jade Ostner, Alex Her, Liz Gelb-O'Connor, John Graham, Tiffany Lee, Zakiya Nashid, Andrew Gadomski, Johnny Campbell, J. T. O'Donnell, Debbie McGrath, China Gorman, Romy Newman, William Tincup, Suzanne Kuhns, Rania Alsawad, Graeme Johnson, Dan Dombey, Dina Medeiros, Shane Gray.